VOLUNTARY WORK

HILARY SEWELL

Published by the
Central Bureau for Educational Visits & Exchanges
in cooperation with the
National Council for Voluntary Organisations

FOURTH EDITION

Distributed in the UK and worldwide by the
Central Bureau for Educational Visits & Exchanges
Seymour Mews, London W1H 9PE, England
Telephone 01-486 5101   Telex 21368 CBEVEX G

Exclusively distributed in mainland Europe by
Gesellschaft fur Internationale Jugendkontakte
eV, Postfach 20 05 62, 5300 Bonn 2, Federal Republic of
Germany   Telephone 0228-322649

ISBN 0 900087 60 9

Typeset, printed and bound in England by
David Green Printers Ltd,
Kettering, Northamptonshire

CONTENTS

SECTION I

OVERSEAS VOLUNTARY SERVICE: RECRUITING AGENCIES

47	Franciscan Volunteer Community
48	Friends of Israel Educational Trust
49	Frontier Apostolate
50	Frontiers Foundation/Operation Beaver
51	Gap Activity Projects (GAP) Ltd
52	German Leprosy Relief Association
53	Girl Guides Association (UK)
54	Green Deserts Ltd
55	Habitat for Humanity Inc
56	Help the Aged
57	Indian Volunteers for Community Service
58	Innisfree Village
59	Institute of Cultural Affairs
61	Intercultural Educational Programmes
62	International Liaison
63	International Voluntary Service
65	International Voluntary Services Inc
66	Jinja Groups Trust
67	Jongeren Vrijwilligers Corps
68	Lalmba Association
69	Lanka Jatika Sarvodaya Shramadana Sangamaya
70	Lay Volunteers International Association
71	Medical Missionary Association
72	Methodist Church Overseas Division
73	Mission Aviation Fellowship
74	Missions to Seamen
75	National Council of YMCAs
76	People-to-People Health Foundation Inc
77	Project Trust
78	Quaker Peace and Service
79	Reggio Terzo Mundo
80	Richmond Fellowship
81	Salvation Army Service Corps
82	SIM International
83	South American Missionary Society
84	TEAR Fund
85	United Kingdom Foundation for the Peoples of the South Pacific
86	United Nations Association International Service
87	United Nations Volunteers
89	United Reformed Church
90	United Society for the Propagation of the Gospel
91	Universities' Educational Fund for Palestinian Refugees
92	Viatores Christi
93	Voluntary Service Overseas
95	Volunteer Missionary Movement
96	World Community Development Service
97	Youth Exchange Centre

SECTION II

OVERSEAS VOLUNTARY SERVICE: ADVISORY BODIES

SECTION III

OVERSEAS PROFESSIONAL RECRUITMENT

SECTION IV

VOLUNTARY SERVICE IN THE UK & IRELAND: RECRUITING AGENCIES

SECTION V

VOLUNTARY SERVICE IN THE UK & IRELAND: ADVISORY BODIES

SECTION VI

PRACTICAL INFORMATION

SECTION VII

INDEXES

The Central Bureau is grateful to
Earthscan and Voluntary Service Overseas
for permission to use their photographs throughout this guide.

Cover: Sierra Leone (Bridget Runcie/VSO)
Title page: Sudan (Caroline Penn/VSO)
7: The Sahara (Mark Edwards/Earthscan)
9: Ethiopia (Mark Edwards/Earthscan)
60: Bombay, India (Mark Edwards/Earthscan)
64: Bahunipati, Nepal (Mark Edwards/Earthscan)
94: Bangladesh (L Summers/VSO)
98: Kashmir (Mark Edwards/Earthscan)
138: South India (Mark Edwards/Earthscan)
144: Niger (Mark Edwards/Earthscan)
150: Chhattera, Haryana, India (Mark Edwards/Earthscan)

The Earthscan photographs are from a series illustrating a number of
important Third World issues, and are available as postcards
from Earthscan, 3 Endsleigh Street, London WC1H 0DD
Tel 01-388 9541.

This guide is published by the Central Bureau for Educational Visits & Exchanges in cooperation with the National Council for Voluntary Organisations.

The Central Bureau for Educational Visits & Exchanges was established in 1948 by the British Government to act as the national information office and coordinating unit for every type of educational visit and exchange. Its main task is the enrichment of the British education system through international contact and cooperation; in-service training abroad and exchanges for teachers, educational administrators, inspectors and advisers; the appointment of foreign language teaching assistants to schools and colleges in the UK and of English language assistants abroad; the placement of students and graduates in training positions in industry and commerce in the UK and abroad; the linking of all types of educational establishment and the twinning of local municipalities, metropolitan authorities and counties with counterparts abroad; the organisation of bi-national and international meetings, conferences, seminars and courses; and the publication of authoritative guides on international education. The Bureau is responsible to the Department of Education & Science, the Scottish Education Department and the Department of Education for Northern Ireland, and also acts in an advisory capacity to other agencies and governments.

Central Bureau for Educational Visits & Exchanges

Seymour Mews, London W1H 9PE Tel 01-486 5101 Telex 21368 CBEVEX G

3 Bruntsfield Crescent, Edinburgh EH10 4HD Tel 031-447 8024

16 Malone Road, Belfast BT9 5BN Tel 0232-664418/9

The National Council for Voluntary Organisations is a politically independent charity which acts as the leading advisory, representative and development agency for voluntary organisations, community groups, pressure groups and charities in England. Its overriding concern is to promote independent, voluntary action within a framework of dynamic, welfare pluralism.

National Council for Voluntary Organisations 26 Bedford Square, London WC1B 3HU Tel 01-636 4066

The British Volunteer Programme is made up of four organisations sending volunteers to developing countries — Catholic Institute for International Relations Overseas Programme, International Voluntary Service, United Nations Association International Service, Voluntary Service Overseas — and Returned Volunteer Action, the independent association of volunteers and ex-volunteers, and the Overseas Development Administration, which provides the government support and liaison; in this guide **BVP** identifies these member organisations. There is also a coordinating secretariat and an advisory council, which makes decisions concerning the running of the programme and volunteer conditions.

British Volunteer Programme, 22 Coleman Fields, London N1 7AG Tel 01-226 6616.

It would be appreciated if returned volunteers would complete and return the report form at the back of this guide.

PREFACE

Since the early 60s, when the British Volunteer Programme was first established in the UK alongside other non-government agencies in Europe and North America, many of which were subsidised by government, our understanding of the role and usefulness of volunteers in the developing countries of the 'Third World' has changed and developed continually. What began in the first decade as a well-meaning and by no means valueless act of charity with undertones of condescension, grew in the second into an attempt to answer the need for special skills, as the developing world became more aware of both its own priorities and of the need to develop by a process of multiplication the technical and professional skills of its indigenous populations. The generalist volunteer was increasingly less in demand than the specialist, and the experienced than the newly qualified. With the third decade, increasing understanding, exemplified in the Brandt Report*, of the economic interdependence of the more developed countries and those in the process of development, many of them still below even the lowest poverty-line, has led to a reappraisal of the role of volunteers and their relationship to those whom they aim to serve, as well as to the searching scrutiny of the projects to which they go. With this has come greater understanding that without the partnership and willing cooperation of agencies, officials and individuals in the country in which projects are established, volunteers and indeed development aid generally may be distorting and harming the very development we would hope to foster and interfering intolerably with the right of the societies in question to determine their own destiny. As a result, most European organisations sponsoring volunteers are seeking a closer involvement of their Third World partners in all aspects of their work.

To argue, as some have done, that

volunteer aid for development is outdated and that such benefit as accrues from it comes in terms of personal experience for the volunteers, is to ignore the vital importance of personal contacts for the growth of mutual understanding and the transmission of skills. In this greater mutual understanding lies the best hope for a real improvement in human happiness worldwide; and the witness of returned volunteers in their own community is or should be a leaven, without which mutual understanding will be increasingly replaced by self-interest and protectionism.

My twenty five years of close personal involvement with volunteers and volunteer agencies both in the UK and in Europe and America leaves me in no doubt that what they provide is both more effective and less wastefully expensive than most other forms of development aid. That the developing world needs and welcomes volunteers, even though it mostly fails to understand their motivation is clear from the continued and, alas, often unfilled demands made to the sending agencies. We might do well to adopt as an explanation of their role the now popular French alternative and call them *cooperants*; but I can assure any volunteer who has the skills and the will to do his or her stint that, with average luck, it will be something not to be missed. As this guide shows, the range of agencies large and small is immensely varied; but there is a lot to learn as well as to give and the best volunteers are those who start with an open mind and an open heart.

Peter Mason

Peter Mason MBE
Formerly Chairman, British Volunteer Programme, and Regional Conference on International Voluntary Service

*The Brandt Report is the result of a unique and independent investigation, commenced in 1976, by a commission of eighteen international statesmen and leaders from many spheres, headed by Willy Brandt, into the urgent problems of inequality in the world and the failure of its economic system. They agreed a set of recommendations including a new approach to international finance and development of the monetary system, and proposed long-term reforms by the year 2000. Published by Pan Books as North-South: A Programme for Survival, *taking its title from the belief that major international initiatives are needed if mankind is going to survive. For the hundreds of millions of people who live on the edge of starvation in the developing countries, the South, this is a matter of fact, but the industrialised countries, the North, have been unwilling in the past to go very far towards accepting the South's case that the world economy works to the South's disadvantage. The Report argues that today, in almost every field of the world's present troubles, a substantial number of the solutions depend on recognising the mutual interests between North and South. It is a political report, and deals with the world problems politically, and calls on all countries to make an imaginative response.*

TO BE A VOLUNTEER

Voluntary service involves commitment; the ideas and attitudes of volunteering once expressed as *helping those less fortunate than ourselves* or as *giving benefits to people in need* are at best inappropriate and at worst patronising. Projects are essentially mutually rewarding and beneficial; both volunteer and co-worker are expected to be enriched by the experience of working on a common task and to have contributed positively, even if fractionally to the betterment of mankind.

The motivations for voluntary service may be many and mixed, but whatever they are potential volunteers must be absolutely clear, positive and honest with themselves about the reasons for volunteering:

Are you running away from unemployment/job/personal problems? Do you feel voluntary service will give you experience and improve career prospects? Have you felt a call from God? Have you a political conviction or commitment to the struggle of exploited peoples? Why are *you* in a position to volunteer?

Considering the importance of the answer, the question of why one is volunteering is often passed over by volunteer and sending agency alike. The volunteer may find difficulty in answering, and there may not be a clear-cut answer, but the process of examining the reasons for even thinking about volunteering is a vital one. For those considering volunteering in the Third World, their understanding of why those countries are underdeveloped needs careful examination:

Why are there people in need who have to rely on other people's voluntary actions? How do the people of such countries come to be so poor, badly housed and underfed, and how can the expertise and investment of the advanced nations help?

Why are you particularly considering volunteering overseas? Is it because going abroad is more exciting? Are you heading for the sunshine?

Although it may not be so obvious, the UK has extremes of wealth and poverty, bad housing, illiteracy, high unemployment and an immigrant population which is discriminated against on many levels; working to overcome these problems and their causes is a worthwhile challenge. Voluntary work experience in the UK may make it easier to be accepted as a volunteer overseas, quite apart from the contribution you can make to the welfare of the people.

One thing *is* clear; one or two years spent in voluntary service is a considerable slice of one's life and it is far too valuable to waste. For such an investment of time and energy it is essential that there is a clear understanding of what volunteers expect and what is expected of them. The *Handbook for Development Workers Overseas* poses a number of questions which volunteers might ask, practical issues that will confront them as each stage of the project unfolds, and suggests that too often volunteers do not ask the key questions either of themselves or of the agencies which engage them.

Which agency?
To aid the prospective volunteer, information on the agencies in this guide has been provided in a set format, providing details on the organisation's origins, background, general orientation and philosophy, countries of operation, opportunities available for voluntary service, personal qualities and qualifications required, length and terms of service, orientation and debriefing

provided, and relevant literature. The volunteer's personal motivation should not be too much at odds with the general aims of the selected sending agency.

The agencies will ask volunteers about their background, competence, views and intentions; volunteers have an equal right to ask the agencies about theirs, and they owe it to themselves, the organisation and most importantly to the people they will be working with to ensure that they are well informed. They should talk to representatives, ask to see field reports, and meet returned volunteers who will provide information based on personal experience.

When a potential agency has been identified - be it commercial, governmental, religious or technical - the volunteer should request further information on its background and philosophy, details of aims and objectives, its scale of operation, the type of enterprise, how it is run, and its support system both in the UK and overseas. Many agencies recruit volunteers on behalf of organisations overseas and so will not themselves be in control of the project volunteers will be working on. The agency should be honest enough to provide prospective volunteers with details of the problems to be encountered, the projects that failed and the basic dilemmas still unresolved after years of activity, as well as the successes. Agencies operating in the Third World should offer their views on underdevelopment and some guidance for the volunteer. The volunteer will be anxious to be selected, but should remember that selection is a two-way process; as much caution should be shown to the agency as they will show to the volunteer. In this guide **BVP** denotes those agencies which are members of the British Volunteer Programme.

Which country?

The countries of operation are listed in each entry and additionally there is a Countries Index. However it must be stressed that many agencies take the view that volunteers should be prepared to serve where they are needed, their own choice of country being of secondary importance. If they have a specific preference they should state this when applying and give their reasons. Questions volunteers should ask regarding the proposed country include its location, climate, and historical and current political situation:

Where in the world is the country? Could you cope with the heat, the dust, the mosquitoes, the lack of basic facilities? Could you come to terms with the practices and the customs of the host community? Are the priorities of the government of the country the same as those of the majority of the people? If not, why not, and what as a volunteer can you or will you, do?

Work assignments

Brief details are provided in each entry of the projects together with the type of personnel required and the number of volunteers recruited annually. The Projects Index identifies the main areas of work in which agencies operate: health care and medicine; engineering and technical services; building and construction; water technology; agriculture, horticulture and fisheries; forestry, environment and conservation; education; community and social service; child care and youth work; management and administration; crafts and small industries; media and publishing; pastoral, theological and evangelical; and the year between, and allows easy identification of prospective agencies.

Volunteers should ask key questions of their proposed work assignment, for example: Why was the project chosen to work on? How does it relate to local needs? Who set it up and finances it? What do the duties entail? Who would you report to? How are decisions reached? Why does the project need the skills of a volunteer? Whose interests will your presence promote? How interested is the recruiting agency in the work you will be doing? If the project is well established volunteers should be shown the field reports and debriefing records of previous volunteers. If the project has been successful, they could ask why the agency has not by now trained a local person to fill the post, and in any case, volunteers should check carefully that by going they are not putting a local person out of a job.

'Useful projects spring from the needs and the initiatives of people at the grass roots, projects in which you will be helping those people construct *their* self-development. At its best, the volunteer contribution, however skilled or technical, is quite different from both professional expertise and straightforward aid, being based on principles of democracy and equality instead of profit or charity' *Thinking about Volunteering*

Personal qualities
Qualifications, however impressive, are not just useless without the right personal qualities, but potentially dangerous.
VSO looks for people who are above all able to communicate. They must be sensitive, patient, resourceful, psychologically and physically robust, and with a good sense of humour. They must want to learn and to make friends. Frank Judd, when Director of Voluntary Service Overseas.

Prospective volunteers should take careful note of the personal qualities requested in each agency's entry, and in addition ask of themselves, for example:

Do I get on with people? Am I prepared to learn from the community I will work in? Can I work as part of a team? Can I cope with isolation? What do I hope to gain? How can I bridge the gap between what the project will expect of me and what I am? Could I learn the language? Have I got communication skills?

Qualifications
In each entry the qualifications, skills and experience required by the agency are outlined. Any nationality restrictions and language requirements are specified, together with projects where spouse/dependents are accepted. **HVC** is used to denote where handicapped volunteers are considered; in all cases consideration to the handicapped will be given, and will be based on the degree of handicap and the project concerned.

Length of service
This guide covers medium (3-12 months) and long-term (1-3+ years) voluntary service; the minimum and maximum periods of service are given for each entry. For short-term voluntary service opportunities, in the UK and overseas, see the companion guide *Working Holidays*.

Conditions of service
Most agencies provide accommodation, board, travel, remuneration and insurance, and details are given under each entry; where costs are paid by the volunteer, information on sponsorship may be given, and this is indicated. Some agencies additionally provide allowances covering equipment, settlement/resettlement, dependents and holidays. It should be ascertained how the volunteer is to be paid and by whom, how social security and pension rights are affected and details of insurance provision. Under what scheme and for what eventualities are you insured? Who will be concerned should you fall ill or have an accident? Where are the nearest medical facilities? General information on these points is

provided in the Practical Information section.

The prospective volunteer should also enquire about job security; volunteers may find themselves doing a completely different job from the one expected, or no work at all, and they will need to know who they can turn to in such an event. They should be clearly informed of the project and what is expected of them. The political climate in some countries is not always stable, and volunteers should establish what security provisions and support they can count on in the case of political or social conflict. It should also be established what happens if, in exceptional circumstances, the volunteer has to leave the project early.

Briefing
Some preparation is obviously needed, and it is in the volunteer's interest to request adequate preparation before setting out. Any agency with a sense of responsibility will make time and find funds for proper training; not all training should be done before leaving, but should be a continuing process carried on at intervals throughout the period of service and include some preparation for the return home. The period of orientation should be long enough to allow the volunteer to take in and digest the information. Volunteers may be living and working in a society where much will be strange and different, and the training is basically to help them understand and cope; they may wish to question the explanations provided for the differences:

Does the training present underdevelopment as something which only occurs in other parts of the world or does it take up questions of poverty and inequality in our own society? What arrangements are there to meet other volunteers and discuss and evaluate their context in the development of the community?

Language is vital if the volunteer is to make contact with ordinary people, and even in countries where English is an official language only a small proportion of the population will speak it; the agency should provide at least basic language instruction. Volunteers should receive up-to-date and relevant technical advice, and be made aware of the social and human effects of any technology introduced. Where compulsory orientation/training and debriefing courses are provided, this is detailed in the agency's entry, but where training is not provided see under Practical Information.

Application
Before applying for any project prospective volunteers should check carefully that what they have to offer matches up to the agency's requirements. Requests for information should be addressed to the contact specified, accompanied by a statement of what the prospective volunteer wants to do and why, and a curriculum vitae. There may be a lengthy period between acceptance and actual assignment to a post, especially if it is overseas; early application is advised in all cases. A stamped addressed envelope should be enclosed with all requests, or in the case of an organisation overseas, an addressed envelope and International Reply Coupons, which are available from post offices.

Handbook for Development Workers Overseas Glyn Roberts. The questions you need to ask plus basic information. Invaluable for all those going abroad as volunteers.

Thinking about Volunteering Introductory handbook for those considering volunteering overseas. Contains a checklist of questions to ask any sending agency and an introduction on volunteering and its place in development.

Both available from Returned Volunteer Action, 1 Amwell Street, London EC1R 1UL Tel 01-278 0804.

SECTION I

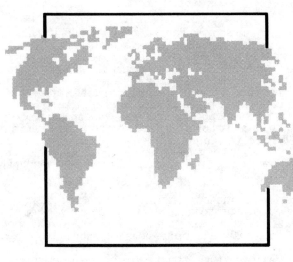

OVERSEAS VOLUNTARY SERVICE
RECRUITING AGENCIES

ACTION HEALTH 2000

Address 35 Bird Farm Road, Fulbourn, Cambridge CB1 5DP
Tel Cambridge 880194

Contact The Director

Countries India; placements in Bangladesh, Sri Lanka imminent.
Possible extension of operations into Kenya and Zaire.

Organisation Founded in 1982, an international voluntary health
association with no political or religious affiliations, working for better
health care in the Third World by creating greater awareness of the
issues involved and giving practical support to appropriate health
programmes. The general purpose of the association is to work towards
the World Health Organisation's target of making basic health care
accessible to the world's poorest peoples. In addition, Action Health 2000
provides and encourages links between health professionals in the
developed and developing countries, and is concerned with health care
research and education.

Opportunities The International Study and Training Programme allows
doctors, nurses, midwives, health visitors and, possibly, other health
personnel to work as volunteers mainly in rural, semi-rural or deprived
urban areas. Recruits 20 health professionals annually.

Personal qualities Applicants should be resourceful, resilient, sensitive
to local cultures and difficulties, compassionate and understanding, and
have non-verbal communication skills. A multi-disciplinary approach and
the ability to work as part of a team required.

Age 18+

Qualifications Appropriate professional health qualifications necessary.
No experience necessary on application, though selected individuals may
be asked to acquire specific experience before being sent overseas.
Volunteers only accepted after satisfactory medical report. All
nationalities considered. **HVC**

Length of service 3 months-2 years

Terms Simple housing, adequate local food, insurance, travel costs and
£30-£50 pocket money per month provided. Participants contribute approx
£750 of total costs, but this and pocket money vary depending on the
project and length of service. Advice given on obtaining sponsorship.

Briefing Shortlisted applicants can meet former volunteers at selection
weekends. Compulsory, comprehensive 3 day orientation course
arranged. Language training may be given. Returned volunteers are
debriefed and provided with help and advice on resettlement and finding
a job, and are encouraged to participate in the society's UK activities.

When to apply Recruitment all year; there is usually a 6-12 month gap
between application and departure.

Publications Newsletter; project reports; information leaflets.

AGENCY FOR PERSONAL SERVICE OVERSEAS

Address 29 Lower Baggot Street, Dublin 2, Ireland Tel Dublin 761571

Contact The Assistant Executive, Overseas Register

Countries Africa: Cameroon, Djibouti, Ethiopia, Gambia, Ghana, Ivory Coast, Kenya, Lesotho, Liberia, Malawi, Mozambique, Nigeria, Rwanda, Sierra Leone, Somalia, Sudan, Swaziland, Tanzania, Uganda, Zambia, Zimbabwe.
Asia: Bangladesh, Bhutan, India, Nepal, Sri Lanka.
Caribbean: Grenada, Jamaica.
Far East: People's Republic of China, Thailand.
Latin America: Brazil, Chile, Ecuador, Peru, Venezuela.
Middle East: Yemen Arab Republic. Pacific: Papua New Guinea.

Organisation A state-sponsored body established in 1974 to promote and sponsor temporary personal service in the developing countries of the world for their economic and social development, in the interests of justice and peace among nations. It co-funds volunteers with other sending agencies and seeks to protect the interests of development workers on their return.

Opportunities Volunteers are needed in the areas of education, medicine, engineering/construction, agriculture, administration and social sciences. There are vacancies for doctors, nurses, radiographers, pharmacists, physiotherapists, nutritionists and medical laboratory technicians; teachers of English, science, maths, primary education, home economics and secretarial/commercial skills; university lecturers; mechanical, civil and electrical engineers; carpenters and builders; horticulturalists, agriculturalists and veterinary surgeons; administrators, secretaries, book keepers and project managers; social workers and community development specialists. Recruits approx 45 volunteers annually.

Personal qualities Applicants must have a genuine interest in helping a developing country.

Age 21+

Qualifications Basic skills or qualifications required.
Experience preferred but not essential. Applicants must be Irish nationals. Knowledge of French language an advantage. **HVC**

Length of service Normally 2 years

Terms Travel and insurance provided; provision of accommodation, meals and pocket money varies according to project/host country.

Briefing Compulsory orientation course arranged. Induction, professional skills and language courses provided.
Re-orientation days/weekends organised in conjunction with Comhlamh, who maintain a job register for returning development workers.

When to apply Recruitment all year.

Publications Annual report.

ALYN

Address POB 9117, Kiryat Hayovel, Jerusalem 91090, Israel Tel 412251

Contact The Coordinator of Voluntary Services

Country Israel

Organisation Founded in 1933, Israel's only long-term orthopaedic hospital and rehabilitation centre for physically handicapped children. A non-profit organisation, providing essential medical and para-medical care, schooling, vocational training and recreational activities. Its objective is to ensure that when youngsters in its care leave, they are equipped with skills and the ability to function in the outside world as productive and, where possible, independent citizens, the programme being geared towards maximising the potential of each child.

Opportunities There are limited vacancies for unskilled volunteers as nurses' aides, working as companions to the children; also for young professionals with hospital-related skills. Tasks involve washing, dressing, feeding, entertaining and accompanying patients on outings. There are nearly 100 children, victims of crippling disease or accident, ranging in age from infancy to young adulthood, most coming from socially/economically deprived families.

Personal qualities Applicants should have a willingness to work with, and help, very physically handicapped children. The work is hard and difficult and often frustrating; understanding, patience, and tolerance are required. Volunteers are an integral part of the hospital team, bringing compassion and understanding to patients undergoing extensive and lengthy treatment.

Age 18/19+

Qualifications No experience needed for nurses' aides, but applicants should be post A level students or equivalent.
Professional posts require relevant skills, qualifications and experience. Knowledge of Hebrew an advantage.

Length of service 6 months minimum, commencing February/March or August/September.

Terms Accommodation provided in small flats in or near the hospital; catering in the staff dining hall. Pocket money £40 per month, £45 after six months, plus ten days paid leave and £40 bonus. Insurance and travel costs paid by the volunteer. 40 hour week, 8 hours per day in shifts.

Briefing Compulsory orientation course arranged at the beginning of service, consisting of lectures and demonstrations, as a basic introduction to working with physically handicapped children, with compulsory weekly lectures.

When to apply Recruitment all year.

Publications *Manual for volunteers*; information leaflets.

AMDOC/OPTION AGENCY

Address Project Concern Universal, PO Box 85322, San Diego, CA 92138, USA Tel 279 9690

Contact The Senior International Placement Counsellor/ Coordinator

Countries Africa: Equatorial Guinea, Ethiopia, Gambia, Ghana, Kenya, Liberia, Malawi, Nigeria, Rwanda, Somalia, Sudan, Uganda.
Asia: Bangladesh, India, Nepal, Pakistan.
Caribbean: Haiti, Jamaica, Puerto Rico, St Lucia, St Vincent, San Salvador.
Far East: Indonesia, Korea, Malaysia, Taiwan, Thailand.
Latin America: Belize, Bolivia, Guatemala, Guyana, Mexico.
Lebanon. USA.

Organisation A non-profit, non-sectarian health care referral and recruitment service founded in 1965, directing professionals into areas of need to benefit medically underserved areas of the world. Annually, over 650,000 patients are treated in developing countries and rural and native America, who would otherwise have little or no access to health care.

Opportunities Vacancies for medical personnel include doctors, nurses, dentists, anaesthetists, therapists, technicians, paediatricians, pharmacists, surgeons, health educators/trainers, midwives, librarians and medical secretaries. There are also vacancies in aquaculture, fisheries, agriculture, forestry, conservation, animal husbandry, and for administration and development generalists.

Personal qualities Volunteers should have a willingness to serve in an area of need, with little compensation.

Qualifications Relevant qualifications, skills and overseas experience required. Knowledge of languages depends on the host country. All nationalities considered. **HVC**

Length of service Short and long-term assignments, ranging from weeks to years.

Terms Food and housing usually provided, and sometimes insurance and travel, depending on organisation/facility.
Short-term volunteers usually receive room and board, and occasionally salary. Long-term volunteers usually receive accommodation, salary and travel assistance. Sponsorship may be provided.

When to apply Recruitment all year.

Publications Bi-monthly newsletter, listing current openings.

ARBEITSGEMEINSCHAFT FUR ENTWICKLUNGSHILFE EV

Address Theodor-Hurth-Strasse 2-6, 5000 Cologne 21, Federal Republic of Germany Tel 815021

Contact The Recruitment Officer

Countries In over 40 countries: Africa, Asia, Far East, Latin America

Organisation Founded in 1959, for all questions concerning development aid through lay volunteers. Composed of the representatives of Catholic organisations, it has dedicated itself to the tasks of ascertaining the personnel demand in general, not only considering overseas demands for volunteers, but also actively looking for opportunities in Europe where volunteers could make a useful contribution. Also recruits, counsels, selects, trains, provides contracts and advises volunteers on reintegration. It believes that wherever the situation demands, constructive and meaningful aid should be given.

Opportunities Volunteers are needed for development work mainly in the medical, agricultural, pastoral and technical fields. Will assist in the procurement of personnel for projects only after priority has been given to local experts. Recruits 100 volunteers annually.

Personal qualities Though no missionary activities are expected from them, applicants should be prepared, through their life and work, to bear witness to what can be considered Christian service in our times.

Age 25+

Qualifications Relevant professional qualifications and experience essential. All nationalities considered. **HVC**

Length of service 3 years

Terms Model contracts have been devised which safeguard living conditions - shelter, living allowance, payments for reintegration and social security - and are applied in such a way as to suit individual situations as adequately as possible. 40 hour week. Travel and insurance costs are met by the projects concerned.

Briefing Preparation for service overseas is provided where necessary by special and further advanced training. Basic orientation seminar held for selection followed by compulsory advanced orientation course. On return assistance in reintegration is provided.

When to apply Recruitment all year.

Publications *Contacts* quarterly magazine; information leaflets.

ARBEITSKREIS FREIWILLIGE SOZIALE DIENSTE DER JUGEND

Address Stafflenbergstrasse 76, 7000 Stuttgart 1, Federal Republic of Germany Tel 2159424

Contact The Bundestutor

Country Federal Republic of Germany

Organisation A Christian organisation coordinating the Voluntary Social Year throughout the Federal Republic, aiming to help society, develop Christianity and widen the experience of the volunteer through practical work and discussions.

Opportunities Volunteers are needed to participate in voluntary social service programmes in homes for the aged, hospitals, kindergarten and children's homes, and with the mentally, socially and physically handicapped. Volunteers are matched increasingly with individuals and families - including disabled, elderly and mentally handicapped people, families needing practical help to stay together, children and young people with special needs, and the terminally ill - needing a high level of support to enable them to live in their own home instead of an institution. There are also opportunities to work with the immigrant population. Volunteers become members of a group, planning and evaluating their work together.

Personal qualities Applicants should have a Christian commitment to community work, prepared to participate fully in their placement by working and learning with others, and be sound in body and mind.

Age 17-25

Qualifications Experience and qualifications not always necessary. All nationalities considered. Spoken German essential.

Length of service One year usually beginning between August and October, but shorter periods can be arranged.

Terms Board, lodging, DM200 pocket money per month and insurance provided. Five weeks holiday per year.

Briefing Orientation seminars with ex-volunteers held before and during the placement to give an idea of the work involved and to discuss expectations, experiences, problems and relevant themes and topics. Debriefing and evaluation arranged.

When to apply Recruitment all year.

Publications Information leaflets, including list of organisations throughout the Federal Republic recruiting volunteers.

ASSOCIATES OF MILL HILL MISSIONARIES

Address St Joseph's College, Lawrence Street, Mill Hill, London NW7 4JX
Tel 01-959 3222

Contact The Vicar General

Countries Africa: Cameroon, Kenya, Sudan, Uganda, Zaire.
Asia: India, Pakistan.
Far East: Indonesia, Malaysia.
Latin America: Brazil, Chile, Falkland Islands, Peru.
Pacific: New Zealand, Philippines.

Organisation The work of the Mill Hill Missionaries goes back to the late 19th century and since 1970 associate lay members have joined the service to work with the priests and brothers. The organisation enables lay missionaries to use their talents and skills to build up God's people in mission lands, and to channel and employ the gifts of many for the service of the missionary ideal.

Opportunities Vacancies exist in the areas of teaching, nursing, social and pastoral work, catechitics, engineering and building work in a missionary context.

Personal qualities Applicants must have Christian and missionary motivation.

Age 21+

Qualifications Relevant qualifications and experience essential. All nationalities considered.

Length of service 3 years

Terms Board and lodging, insurance, travel and allowance provided.

Briefing Compulsory four month preparatory course organised before Associates take up their placements. Short periods of group meetings provided as debriefing.

When to apply Recruitment all year.

Publications Two booklets: *A Century of Charity - The Story of the Mill Hill Missionaries*; *The Changing Face of Mission*.

ATD FOURTH WORLD

Address 48 Addington Square, London SE5 7LB
Tel 01-703 3231

Contact The General Secretary

Countries Africa: Burkina Faso, Central African Republic, Ivory Coast, Reunion, Senegal. Asia: Thailand. North America: Canada, USA. Europe: Belgium, France, Netherlands, Switzerland.

Organisation Aide a Toute Detresse is an international movement founded in 1958 in France, and established as a charity in the UK in 1963. Millions of workers and their families have for generations lived in extreme poverty, increasingly dependent on and controlled by others and despite their hopes and efforts are denied the means of being fully active members of society. In every country, these families constitute the Fourth World – ten million people in Europe alone. ATD works alongside the most disadvantaged and excluded families, as well as with all levels in society, to protect and guarantee the fundamental rights of families to family life, education and representation.

Opportunities Workcamps and working weekends are arranged, where volunteers work alongside members of the permanent voluntariat, doing building, decorating, gardening, secretarial and translation work at centres and homes. For volunteers who are able to stay longer, it is sometimes possible to take part in projects at nurseries, skill centres, libraries, youth and children's clubs and on family holidays as an introduction to the permanent voluntariat.

Personal qualities Applicants should have a genuine interest in learning about the experiences and hopes of very disadvantaged communities as a vital first step to building a future with them, and a willingness to work hard with others as a team.

Age 18+

Qualifications There are no minimum requirements, professionally or academically; everyone is welcome, including couples with families. Knowledge of local languages useful. All nationalities considered. **HVC**

Length of service An open-ended commitment is preferred if intending to become a member of the permanent voluntariat.

Terms Volunteers on workcamps/working weekends contribute approx £3 per day towards food and accommodation. Permanent voluntariat members are provided with accommodation, food, pocket money after three months service and a minimum wage after one year. Accident insurance provided.

Briefing Volunteers receive a full introduction to the work of ATD; evaluation and debriefing sessions are arranged.

When to apply Recruitment all year through national offices.

Publications *Fourth World Journal* and *Fourth World Youth Newsletter*; Annual Report; plus numerous Fourth World books.

AUXILIARY MISSIONARIES OF THE ASSUMPTION

Address Assumption Convent, 227 N Bowman Avenue, Merion, PA 19066, USA Tel 664 3074

Contact The General Councillor

Countries West and East Africa. Far East: Japan.
Latin America: Argentina, Brazil, Mexico. Pacific: Philippines.

Organisation Founded in 1960, provides lay women with the opportunity of giving their skills to others in teaching, medical work or towards the development of peoples in a foreign country.

Opportunities Volunteers are needed as teachers at elementary and secondary level, and in community and social development.

Personal qualities Volunteers need generosity, forgetfulness of self and the willingness to tackle any job they are given.
They should also have a spiritual dimension in their lives and high moral standards, plus an appreciation of other points of view and cultures.

Age 21-50

Qualifications College graduates or equivalent preferred.
Volunteers should have had work experience during their school life; a second language is helpful. Preferably, applicants should be single females without dependents. **HVC**

Length of service 1 year minimum.

Terms Room and board provided varies according to the host country. Volunteers receive pocket money and the cost of one way fare for a one year commitment; return fare paid for a two year commitment.

Briefing Orientation course arranged prior to departure.

When to apply Apply by 1 June

BALKAN-JI-BARI INTERNATIONAL

Address Association for Child and Youth Welfare of the World, Bapu Gaon, Via Dahanu Road, 401602 Maharashtra, India
Tel Bombay 532008

Contact The Executive Director

Country India

Organisation Founded in 1923 Children's Own Garden International promotes the welfare of children and young people worldwide. The main objectives are to make children as happy as possible and to give them scope to develop by themselves; to promote the inherent rights, education and well-being of all children in home, school and community; to bring into active cooperation all individuals and groups concerned with children; and to encourage the continuous growth of workers, voluntary and professional, to carry on children's activities. To achieve these objectives, it is guided by a dynamic philosophy of education through recreation which is flexible and responsive to human needs in a changing society.

Opportunities Volunteers are needed to look after children's education and recreation, helping out with office work, and carrying out youth activities.

Personal qualities Applicants must have energy, enthusiasm and a real desire for social service, generally among the poor.

Age 16/18+

Qualifications Experience not necessary as it can be gained by working. Knowledge of English and Hindustani desirable. All nationalities considered. **HVC**

Length of service 6 months minimum, mid-June to April.

Terms Simple accommodation and vegetarian food provided. Travel, insurance and pocket money supplied by the volunteer. 28-30 hour week. Participants are encouraged to obtain sponsorship.

Briefing Orientation course provided. Advice/debriefing may be provided on completion, according to work undertaken.

When to apply Recruitment all year.

Publications Information leaflets.

BIBLE AND MEDICAL MISSIONARY FELLOWSHIP INTERNATIONAL

Address Whitefield House, 186 Kennington Park Road, London SE11 4BT
Tel 01-735 8227

Contact The Personnel Secretary

Countries Asia: Bangladesh, Bhutan, Central Asia, India, Nepal, Pakistan
Middle East: Bahrain, Jordan, Kuwait, Lebanon, Qatar

Organisation Founded in 1852 and radically updated through changes of
name and function, BMMF is a modern mission serving the people of Asia
and the Middle East. In proclaiming the gospel its members seek the
salvation of individuals, the building of the Church and the meeting of
human need to the glory of God. Interdenominational in structure,
evangelical in doctrine, the provision of medicine, education, literature,
pastoral and evangelistic work continue to be its main tasks.
Activity also extends into theological training, sensitive development of
initiatives in Muslim areas and relief teams for areas of acute human
crisis.

Opportunities Health care vacancies for doctors, midwives, pharmacists,
nurses, surgeons, paediatricians, opthalmologists, physiotherapists,
anaesthetists, dentists and community health programme workers.
Technical specialists are required in agriculture, animal husbandry,
forestry, irrigation, engineering and maintenance. Teaching opportunities
include primary/elementary, English as a second language, with the blind
and mentally handicapped, adult literacy and in-service training.
Specialists are also needed in the creation of cottage industries,
publishing, translation, administration, accountancy, evangelism and
pastoral work.

Personal qualities Applicants must be committed Christians, have a
sense of divine calling which will sustain even when the work may seem
professionally unrewarding, a desire and ability to communicate on
spiritual matters, perseverance and adaptability to new situations.

Age 23+

Qualifications Relevant professional qualifications and experience
essential. Applicants must be recommended by their local church. All
nationalities considered. Good knowledge of English necessary.

Length of service 3 years minimum.

Terms Accommodation, travel, insurance and allowance provided.
Through team support the volunteer and BMMF raise the necessary
funds.

Briefing After interview a correspondence study programme is followed
by compulsory weekend orientation. Ten day orientation on arrival. Close
contact maintained throughout with advice and support given on return.

When to apply Recruitment all year.

Publications *Go* magazine; *Call to Prayer* year book; information leaflets.

THE BIBLE CHURCHMEN'S MISSIONARY SOCIETY

Address 251 Lewisham Way, London SE4 1XF Tel 01-691 6111

Contact The General Secretary

Countries Africa: Kenya, Tanzania, Uganda.
Europe: Portugal, Spain. Latin America: Bolivia, Peru.

Organisation Founded in 1922 to lead men and women to personal faith in Christ and to build them up in the fellowship of His church, working at all times in partnership with overseas churches.

Opportunities Requests from overseas churches are for accountants, administrators, agriculturalists, Bible teachers, evangelists, primary and secondary teachers, doctors, student workers, and people skilled in broadcasting, bookselling and literature production.

Personal qualities Volunteers should have a commitment to Jesus Christ as Saviour and Lord, a sense of God's call and a willingness to work in partnership with the overseas church as a dedicated servant of God.

Age 21+; most volunteers are in their late 20s

Qualifications Qualifications and experience in appropriate field needed. Professional and often postgraduate qualifications needed for medical and teaching personnel. Knowledge/study of languages required as appropriate. All nationalities considered.

Length of service 2 years minimum.

Terms Most overseas institutions and dioceses provide basic accommodation but not food. Monthly allowance is designed to provide a reasonable standard of living. National Insurance contributions and travel provided.

Briefing Participants should have had training at All Nations Christian College or a similar institution.
Consultation with one of the Area Secretaries provided as debriefing.

When to apply Recruitment all year.

Publications *Mission* quarterly magazine; *On The Move* newsletter.

BRETHREN VOLUNTEER SERVICE

Address 1451 Dundee Avenue, Elgin, IL 60120, USA Tel 742 5100

Contact The Recruitment Officer

Countries Caribbean: Haiti, Puerto Rico, Virgin Islands.
Europe: France, Federal Republic of Germany, Ireland, Netherlands, Northern Ireland, Poland, Switzerland.
Latin America: Bolivia, Chile, Ecuador, El Salvador, Honduras, Mexico, Nicaragua, Uruguay.
People's Republic of China; Egypt; Israel; USA.

Organisation A Christian service programme founded in 1948, dedicated to advocating justice, peacemaking and serving basic human needs. BVS is characterised by the spirit of sharing God's love through acts of service and reflects the heritage of reconciliation and service of the Church of the Brethren, its sponsoring denomination.

Opportunities Over 200 projects some dealing with immediate needs, others working towards changing unjust systems; the range of personnel is wide and constantly updated. Recent projects have needed agricultural workers, environmentalists, maintenance experts, construction supervisors, writers, drivers, cooks, craft workers, medical personnel, child care aides, social/youth workers, community organisers, instructors to the disabled, aides to the aged, peace/prison reform organisers, refugee resettlement coordinators, teachers and administrators.

Personal qualities Applicants should be willing to act on their commitments and values; they will be challenged to offer themselves, their time and talents, to work that is both difficult and demanding. They are expected to study and examine the Christian faith, to be open to personal growth and willing to share in the lives of others.

Age 18+

Qualifications High school education or equivalent required.
The programme especially needs those with relevant skills and experience, but also the less experienced if they bring a willingness to grow and a desire to serve. All nationalities considered. **HVC**

Length of service 1 year minimum for USA; 2 years service overseas.

Terms Participants meet their own costs to orientation in the USA; thereafter BVS provides travel, insurance and $35 per month allowance, v ch may be increased in the second year.
B ard and lodging provided in apartments/houses or occasionally with a family.

Briefing Compulsory 3 week orientation course when project assignments are made with the input of BVS and the volunteer.
There may be a waiting period between orientation and overseas assignment; interim assignments will be arranged. Debriefing provided during in-service retreat.

When to apply Minimum 3 months in advance.

Publications *Project* quarterly booklet; information leaflets.

BRITISH EXECUTIVE SERVICE OVERSEAS

Address 10 Belgrave Square, London SW1X 8PH Tel 01-235 0991

Contact The Administrator

Countries Eastern and Southern Africa, Mauritius, Seychelles; India; Malaysia; Pacific Islands.

Organisation An independent organisation, initiated by the Institute of Directors and established with the backing of the British Government and the Confederation of British Industry.
The aims of the scheme are the advancement of industrial and commercial training and education in developing countries; the improvement of managerial skills leading to greater efficiency in industry and commerce in these countries; and the promotion of the science of supervisory management and organisation of systems and methods in the fields of industry, trade and commerce. BESO recruits executives by enlisting the help of employers, federations, professional institutes and trade associations, and maintains a register of executives.

Opportunities Businessmen with industrial and commercial backgrounds are sent to advise small and medium-sized businesses in developing countries on specific problems, to share knowledge and expertise in a practical way with indigenous businesses and to help those countries achieve economic independence, self-sustaining growth and a higher standard of living.

Personal qualities Applicants should have a commitment to passing on their skills in developing countries.

Qualifications Volunteers should be retired businessmen or executives on secondment from their employers, with a successful record in the industrial or commercial fields. The level of expertise required depends on individual assignment.

Length of service Average period 2-3 months; maximum is usually 6 months.

Terms Travel, insurance and incidental expenses of the volunteer and spouse are met by BESO. Accommodation, subsistence and local transportation are borne by the requesting organisation.

Briefing Briefing provided on local conditions.

When to apply Recruitment all year.

Publications Information leaflets.

BUREAU FOR OVERSEAS MEDICAL SERVICE

Address Africa Centre, 38 King Street, London WC2E 8JT
Tel 01-836 5833

Contact The Administrator

Countries Recent vacancies have arisen in the following countries.
Africa: Egypt, Ethiopia, Ghana, Guinea-Bissau, Kenya, Liberia, Malawi,
Mozambique, Nigeria, Seychelles, Sierra Leone, Sudan, Tanzania,
Transkei, Uganda, Zaire, Zambia, Zimbabwe.
Asia: Bangladesh, Bhutan, India, Maldives, Nepal, Pakistan.
Caribbean: Grenada, Nevis. Far East: Indonesia, Malaysia, Thailand.
Latin America: Brazil. Middle East: Lebanon, United Arab Emirates.
Pacific: Aboriginal freehold lands of Central Australia, Fiji,
Papua New Guinea, Philippines, Western Samoa.

Organisation A charity founded in 1980 as a coordinating agency for
experienced health workers. It is not a recruiting agency, but runs a
register for health workers interested in working in the Third World, acts
as a clearing house for a wide range of health posts, and provides
information and advice on working overseas and resettlement. Aims to
eliminate costly communication difficulties for those who can least afford
them, providing a focus for the needy and relating requests to a large
pool of professionals.

Opportunities The register lists health posts, a list of organisations
administering such posts including voluntary, governmental and mission
agencies, and a current list of qualified staff who wish to volunteer. It
includes not only doctors, (general medical officers, surgeons, physicians,
pathologists, anaesthetists, radiologists, paediatricians,
obstetricians/gynaecologists, opthalmologists and cardiologists), but also
health workers such as nurses, midwives, health educators/visitors,
pharmacists, physiotherapists, nutritionists, tutors, occupational therapists,
medical administrators, water engineers and dentists. A large number of
posts are at mission hospitals.

Personal qualities As required by the recruiting agencies.

Qualifications Nurses must be SRN and possess a further qualification in
teaching or have previous Third World experience, as most vacancies
are for nurse tutors. Doctors must be fully recognised in the UK, have
qualifications recognised in the UK or have qualifications necessary for
registration; as applicants must be willing to teach, they should have a
minimum of two years work experience.

Length of service 1-2 years, but occasionally there are opportunities for
periods of a few months.

Terms Contractual details vary according to the recruiting agency, and
are outside the responsibility of BOMS.

When to apply Recruitment all year.

Publications *News and Jobs* bi-monthly newsletter; Annual Report; advice
sheets for doctors and health workers intending to work overseas.

CATHOLIC INSTITUTE FOR INTERNATIONAL RELATIONS

Address CIIR Overseas Programme, 22 Coleman Fields, London N1 7AF
Tel 01-354 0883

Contact The Recruitment Officer

Countries Africa: Somalia, Zimbabwe. Middle East: Yemen Arab Republic.
Latin America: Costa Rica, Ecuador, Honduras, Nicaragua, Peru.

Organisation Founded in 1940, an educational charity providing
information on social, economic and religious affairs in Latin America,
Southern Africa and Asia. CIIR's Overseas Programme is open to people
of any religious belief or none. Technical support is provided for
community projects which tackle the causes of poverty; projects are
identified that promote the interests of the poor in each country. **BVP**

Opportunities Posts are available for agriculturalists, midwives,
pharmacists, physiotherapists, architects, engineers and teachers in
agricultural cooperatives, urban and rural health care schemes, national
development projects, peasant-run educational programmes, educational
institutions and community organisations. Most jobs involve training local
people in new skills.

Personal qualities Applicants should have a keen interest in the host
country, a desire to adapt their skills to a new environment and to share
these skills with, and learn from, their local colleagues.

Age 21+. Most workers are 25-35. There is no upper age limit;
applications from retired people in good health welcome.

Qualifications Recognised professional qualifications or relevant training,
together with post-qualification work experience essential. Spanish or
Arabic useful; two month intensive language courses provided where
necessary. Couples without dependent children welcome provided both
have skills or qualifications acceptable to the programme and can be
posted together. No restrictions on nationality unless imposed by the host
country. Applicants must be available in Britain for interview. **HVC**

Length of service 2 years minimum.

Terms Volunteers receive basic monthly salary related to local incomes,
in the range of $250-$450 to cover the needs of a worker without
dependents, board and accommodation depending on the post, travel,
National Insurance and pension contributions, health and property
insurance, clothing and equipment allowance, mid-term holiday grant and
resettlement grant on completion of contract.

Briefing Selection weekends held throughout the year. Compulsory
orientation course arranged, involving individual research, professional
training sessions and briefing on project details and country background.
Debriefing with the London staff member responsible for the programme.

When to apply Recruitment all year.

Publications *Case Study* series on projects; *Comment* series on particular
countries, regions and other topics; Annual Review.

CENTRAL ASIAN MISSION

Address 166 Tonbridge Road, Maidstone, Kent ME16 8SR
Tel Maidstone 673410

Contact The Administrative Secretary

Countries Asia: Afghanistan, Bangladesh, Bhutan, Nepal, Northern India, Pakistan.

Organisation Founded in 1902, a small, British-based, Protestant evangelical interdenominational mission which supplies missionary personnel to positions throughout Central Asia.

Opportunities There are a wide range of posts for doctors, nurses and midwives, primary and secondary teachers, and for secretaries and administrators. The Mission contributes workers to existing projects in need of help within the national church and in inter-mission groups.

Personal qualities Applicants must be committed Christians who will proclaim the gospel of Jesus Christ whilst at the same time using their professional skills to minister to the practical needs of the people. Only consecrated workers, sound in the fundamental truths of the scriptures and who believe and teach the whole counsel of God, are sent out.

Age No restriction

Qualifications Relevant skills and qualifications required.
Applicants with British nationality preferred, but foreign nationals with a strong sense of mission may also be accepted.

Length of service For life.

Terms An allowance is paid which covers the cost of accommodation and food. Travel costs and insurance provided.

When to apply Recruitment all year.

Publications *Dawn in Central Asia* magazine published three times per year; information leaflets; prayer lists, letters and tapes.

CENTRO LAICI ITALIANI PER LE MISSIONI

Address Via San Antonio 5, 20122 Milan, Italy Tel 805 2076

Contact The Director

Countries Africa: Central African Republic, Ivory Coast, Zambia.

Organisation A Christian voluntary organisation founded in 1954, particularly interested in being a service to families who believe in the evangelical message, and firmly believes that the Church's work does not simply revolve around the community.
Their main objective is the development of the Third World through professional training and agricultural advancement, and lay volunteers are recruited and prepared for work on development projects. By providing medicine and by promoting a health education programme which places emphasis on hygiene and sanitation, they hope to develop an increased awareness and understanding between the differing cultures.

Opportunities A limited number of volunteers are needed to work as doctors, surgeons, hospital attendants, nurses, teachers, agronomists and engineers. Projects include a Zambesi training farm pilot scheme where volunteers pass on their technical and agricultural skills, local women are taught dressmaking and cookery and a pharmacy is administered; and development of the health and social sphere in the Central African Republic through hospital administration, training of local para-medical staff, hygiene and sanitary education, formation of local health care teams, and the initiation of cooperative schemes to provide needs such as drinking water.

Personal qualities Applicants should be able to give a Christian testimony during their service, and have a capacity for relationships with the local population. They should be able to overcome situations that are often difficult.

Age 18+

Qualifications Qualifications essential; experience useful. Knowledge of English and/or French required. All nationalities considered.

Length of service 2 years minimum.

Terms Volunteers live in self-sufficient small groups in houses. Pocket money, travel and insurance provided for Italian nationals only.

Briefing Orientation course arranged, about one year before departure, with the chance to discuss the work of the organisation and its programmes with returned volunteers. Special courses arranged if necessary. Advice and publications provided to returning volunteers.

When to apply Recruitment all year.

Publications *Ad Lucem* quarterly review; information leaflets and publications on Third World problems and international volunteering.

CENTRO STUDI TERZO MONDO

Address Via G B Morgagni 39, 20129 Milan, Italy Tel 2719041

Contact The Director

Countries Africa: Angola, Chad, Ethiopia, Mozambique, Somalia. Asia: India. Far East: Indonesia. Latin America: Brazil, Ecuador, Peru.

Organisation Founded in 1962, the Centre has a wide-ranging involvement with the Third World which includes arranging development projects, organising courses, initiating studies and research, and issuing documentation, books and journals. Also recruit volunteers for other Italian organisations employing volunteers overseas.

Opportunities Volunteers are needed to work as teachers, in the medical and social services, in community work and to organise integrated projects. Recruit 25 volunteers annually.

Personal qualities Applicants should be reliable and have a serious commitment to voluntary work.

Age 18+

Qualifications Qualifications and experience not always necessary but often desirable, depending on the post. All nationalities considered.

Length of service Open ended commitment.

Terms Board and accommodation depends on the country, but usually provided in private houses. Pocket money $100 per week and insurance provided. 36 hour week. Travel costs are met for periods of at least six months service. Advice given to participants on obtaining sponsorship.

Briefing Compulsory orientation course organised for those without qualifications and experience. On return, advice/debriefing meetings organised every two months.

When to apply Recruitment all year.

Publications *Terzo Mondo* quarterly journal; *Quaderni di Terzo Mondo* irregular publication.

CHRISTIAN FOUNDATION FOR CHILDREN

Address 13001 Wornall Road, Kansas City, MO 64145, USA
Tel 941 9100

Contact The Director of Volunteer Services

Countries Latin America: Belize, Brazil, Chile, Colombia, El Salvador, Guatemala, Honduras, Mexico, Venezuela.
Dominican Republic; Philippines; USA.

Organisation Founded in 1981 by former missionaries and lay volunteers, a non-profit, interdenominational organisation dedicated to help overcome hunger, disease, loneliness and suffering by caring for homeless, orphaned, crippled and abandoned children, refugees and the aged. The Foundation provides food, shelter, clothing, medicine, education, vocational and nutritional training, and pastoral and social service to people in need regardless of age, race or creed.

Opportunities Volunteers needed include child care centre workers, health care instructors, nurses, nutritionists, social/community workers, agriculturalists, craft workers, teachers, recreation organisers, house parents, group home staff and secretaries. Health centres and schools for the poor and handicapped, children's clinics, the training of mothers in the production of vegetables and for income producing trades, educational programmes and the provision of children's homes are examples of the support given. Recruit 15-25 volunteers annually.

Personal qualities Applicants should have a strong faith in the Heavenly Father and the equality of the human family, and a sincere desire to help needy children and the aged.

Age 21+

Qualifications Some professional skills preferred, although direct experience is not necessary. Spanish or Portuguese language required. All nationalities considered. **HVC**

Length of service 1 year minimum; longer commitment preferred.

Terms Board and lodging provided on site by the host missionary or coordinator. Travel, insurance and pocket money provided by the volunteer. 40-60 hour week. Advice given on obtaining sponsorship.

Briefing Orientation provided on the mission site. The Foundation stays in contact with the volunteers and, through a sister agency, tries to find employment for them on their return.

When to apply Recruitment all year.

Publications *The Christian Foundation For Children* monthly newsletter.

CHRISTIAN OUTREACH

Address 34 St Mary's Crescent, Leamington Spa, Warwickshire CV31 1JL
Tel Leamington Spa 315301

Contact The Home Director

Countries Philippines; Sudan; Thailand.

Organisation Founded in 1966, a British voluntary agency involved in
relief work by the provision of primary health care in refugee camps and
the support of disadvantaged children in homes.

Opportunities Skilled volunteers are required to help in children's homes
and camps for refugees from Ethiopia and Kampuchea. Nurses, midwives,
nutritionists, engineers, sanitation experts, builders, electricians,
administrators and primary teachers are needed. Work includes the
operation of Mother and Child Health Centres, clinics, community health,
intensive and supplementary feeding programmes, site maintenance and
construction, and education. Conditions can be extremely severe. Recruit
20-25 volunteers annually.

Personal qualities Applicants should have Christian commitment, a
desire to help others and be adaptable.

Age 22+

Qualifications Relevant qualifications required, but previous overseas
experience not essential. All nationalities considered. A good command of
English necessary.

Length of service 1 year contract, renewable.

Terms Volunteers are housed in local accommodation, with meals
prepared by staff. Medical insurance, approx £40 pocket money per
month and travel costs provided.

Briefing Compulsory orientation course arranged. Debriefing sessions
held at weekends as necessary.

When to apply Recruitment all year.

Publications Quarterly newsletter; *Prayer Letter*.

CHRISTIANS ABROAD

Address Livingstone House, 11 Carteret Street, London SW1H 9DL
Tel 01-222 2165

Contact The Secretary for Information

Countries Africa: Kenya, Malawi, Zambia.

Organisation Founded in 1972, an ecumenical body supported by aid and mission agencies providing information and advice on work abroad to help volunteers discover how their skills can be used and which organisations can be approached. An interviewing, appointments and preparation service is provided for over 30 organisations seeking Christians to work abroad.

Opportunities Volunteers are needed to work as secondary teachers of English, mathematics and the sciences, and occasionally as development specialists and health workers, but this varies according to the organisation concerned.

Personal qualities Applicants should have a wish to learn as well as to give, with a genuine desire to become involved in the life of the Church abroad. They should have a willingness to adjust what they know to new situations, an ability to cope with loneliness and frustration, and to respect the expectations of people overseas. Qualifications and experience are more important than age.

Age 21+; varies according to recruiting organisation.

Qualifications Volunteers must have teaching qualifications and experience. Other conditions vary according to the recruiting organisation.

Length of service Mainly 2-3 years; varies according to the employer.

Terms Terms of service vary; accommodation usually provided in flats with self-catering facilities. Salary usually paid, but this also varies: some posts are paid on local terms, and some carry inducement allowances. Travel provided, but not usually insurance.

Briefing Five day briefing course at The Centre for International Briefing can be arranged. Returned volunteers are welcome to arrange for personal advice, but no formal debriefing service is provided.

When to apply Recruitment all year.

Publications *A Place for You Overseas* series of leaflets covering opportunities abroad through a variety of organisations and schemes; *Opportunities Abroad* six-monthly list drawing together current vacancies through approx 30 mission and voluntary organisations; *Christians on the Move* booklet on the experiences of those who have worked abroad; *A Place for You Back in Britain* for returned volunteers.

CHURCH MISSIONARY SOCIETY

Address 157 Waterloo Road, London SE1 8UU Tel 01-928 8681

Contact The Volunteers Secretary

Countries Africa: Burundi, Egypt, Gambia, Kenya, Nigeria, Rwanda, Sierra Leone, Sudan, Tanzania, Uganda, Zaire.
Asia: India, Nepal, Pakistan, Sri Lanka.
Far East: Hong Kong, Japan, Malaysia, Singapore.
Middle East: Bahrain, Israel, Jordan, Lebanon.

Organisation Founded in 1799 in response to Christ's command to proclaim the Good News, a voluntary society set within the worldwide Anglican Communion, which sees its role as a source of interchange, not only of people, with varied skills, experiences and spiritual gifts, but also of material resources, ideas, news and mutual prayer support.

Opportunities CMS responds to a wide variety of requests from overseas churches. Volunteers are needed to work in health care: surgeons, doctors, nurses, paramedicals, trainers of the handicapped and health educationists; in education: heads of schools, teachers, college principals and lecturers; in administration: accountants and secretaries; in rural development: architects, builders, engineers, craftsmen, instructors, technicians; and in Church work: chaplains/pastoral workers, evangelists. Recruits 20-40 volunteers annually.

Personal qualities Applicants should have a positive, growing Christian faith and a desire to share this with others, while working in partnership with an overseas church. They should be flexible, willing to work with others and able to live with frustrations and disappointments.

Age 21+

Qualifications Professional qualification, skills, training and/or experience which can be matched with specific needs in the host country required. Only British residents can be considered. **HVC**

Length of service 2 years minimum, usually departing September or January.

Terms Volunteers are financially supported by the host church, institution or CMS, and often receive an allowance equivalent to that of a similarly qualified national or missionary. In certain locations the volunteer receives board and lodging plus pocket money. Return air fare, medical insurance and National Insurance contributions provided.

Briefing The selection process for potential volunteers culminates in a residential conference. Successful applicants attend a compulsory 2 or 3 week training course or spend a term at missionary training college, depending on the gifts and needs of the individual and the demands of the location. Individual debriefing and reorientation weekend and allowance paid on return.

When to apply Recruitment all year.

Publications Information leaflets.

THE CHURCH OF SCOTLAND, BOARD OF WORLD MISSION AND UNITY

Address 121 George Street, Edinburgh EH2 4YN Tel 031-225 5722

Contact The Deputy General Secretary

Countries Africa: Cross River State, Ghana, Malawi, Nigeria, Sudan, Zambia, Zimbabwe.
Asia: Bangladesh, India, Pakistan.
Middle East: Israel.

Organisation The Board runs the Operation Youth Share scheme, in which young people with some specific skill or professional qualification work with the Church overseas.

Opportunities There are vacancies for teachers, accountants, administrative staff, secretaries, librarians, agriculturalists, doctors, nurses and other medical personnel.

Personal qualities Applicants should have a firm Christian commitment and be willing to serve others.

Age 18+

Qualifications Volunteers should be trained personnel with relevant skills.

Length of service 3-12 months.

Terms Full board and lodging provided. Pocket money provision varies according to the host country. Volunteers are expected to meet their own travel and insurance costs.

When to apply Recruitment all year.

Publications *Life and Work* monthly magazine, a record of the Church of Scotland; *Frontiers* newspaper focusing on world mission and unity; information leaflets and various books.

COMMUNITY FOR CREATIVE NON-VIOLENCE

Address 1345 Euclid Street, NW, Washington, DC 20009, USA
Tel 332 4332

Contact The Personnel Officer

Country USA

Organisation Founded in 1970 to carry out inner city poverty work, providing over 2000 poor and homeless a day with food, shelter, clothing and medical care. It sees the sharing of bread with the victims of injustice as a responsibility born of faith and sees the equivalent need to resist the forces of injustice which victimise all. The Community operates soup kitchens and has opened hospitality and pre-trial houses, a medical clinic and overnight emergency shelters. In pursuit of just action by those, locally and nationally, who possess the needed resources, it has aggressively involved itself in the development of shelter space, food programmes, long-range policy and legislation.

Opportunities Volunteers serve and work with, and learn from, the homeless poor of Washington, living together and existing on donations of food and funds and work full time for the people of the street. Daily life is composed of direct service as well as public education and action directed at both Church and State. While predominantly Christian, the religious make-up of the Community is richly varied; volunteers come from a variety of backgrounds and there is no hierarchy of roles.

Personal qualities Applicants should have a willingness to work hard, live simply and stretch the meaning of their faith to turn beliefs into daily acts. The common thread bringing volunteers together is the recognition of the need to blend within the individual and the community the elements of spirituality, direct service, resistance, constructive programme and the personal integration of justice.

Age No restrictions.

Qualifications No special skills or previous experience necessary. All nationalities considered. Volunteers should be English-speaking.

Length of service Open-ended commitment.

Terms Volunteers share Community households. No pocket money, insurance or travel provided.

When to apply Recruitment all year.

Publications Information leaflets.

COMPAGNONS BATISSEURS

Address rue Notre Dame de Grâces 63, 5400 Marche en Famenne, Belgium Tel 314 413

Contact Responsable en Secteur Long Term

Country Belgium

Organisation Founded in 1977, the Franco-Belgian branch of Internationale Bouworde aims to play an active role in resolving social problems and in improving the living standards of the economically, socially, mentally and physically underprivileged. The organisations that contact Compagnons Batisseurs for help do not request volunteers for purely economic reasons but because the inclusion of voluntary community action is part of the nature of their projects.

Opportunities Volunteers are needed to participate in a wide variety of workcamps as members of international teams. Projects include construction and renovation of homes for families, centres for the handicapped and immigrant communities; working with children, youth, the elderly, village communities and the unemployed; restoring derelict urban areas, schools, churches and farms; and setting up parks and adventure playgrounds. Projects last for 15 days to 1 month. There are also limited opportunities helping with the administrative work of the association. Recruit approx 200 volunteers annually. For short-term opportunities, see *Working Holidays*.

Personal qualities Participants should be willing to accept the aims of the partner organisations and be prepared to contribute practically to work which is in response to the urgent needs of a particular group. They should also be highly motivated, adaptable and able to put up with physical discomfort.

Age 18-30

Qualifications No qualifications or experience required; plumbing, carpentry, sanitation and electrical skills an advantage. Most nationalities considered.

Length of service 3 months-2 years

Terms Food, basic accommodation, insurance and FB600 per week pocket money provided. Travel costs are not paid. 7 hour day, 5 day week. Registration fee FB900.

When to apply Recruitment all year.

Publications *L'etancon dur* periodical; information leaflets.

DANCHURCHAID

Address 3 Sankt Peders Straede, 1453 Copenhagen K, Denmark
Tel 152800

Contact The Secretary, Department for Overseas Staff

Countries Africa: Ethiopia, Sudan, Tanzania, Uganda.
Asia: Bangladesh, India, Pakistan, Sri Lanka.
Latin America: Bolivia, Nicaragua.

Organisation Founded in 1922, Danchurchaid is the largest private relief organisation in Denmark. It is not specifically concerned with missionary work; recipients of aid are not subject to conditional demands for membership of any particular religious community. The overall principle is to help where help is needed. Requests for over half the assistance to projects and emergency situations are channelled through the Lutheran World Federation and the World Council of Churches.

Opportunities The majority of projects are for long-term development aimed at increasing health care provision, getting food production going, developing the possibilities for education, helping with vocational training and small-scale industries, endeavouring to relieve social distress for the physically handicapped and offering legal aid and assistance to those subject to violations of human rights. Recruit 15-20 volunteers annually.

Personal qualities Applicants should be committed to the goals of Danchurchaid. Volunteers will often hold senior positions, so a level-headed approach and the ability to take a comprehensive view of matters is needed.

Age 25+

Qualifications Relevant qualifications are required plus at least two years' experience after graduation. Knowledge of the Third World particularly through work or travel is desirable.
All nationalities considered. English language required for most jobs.

Length of service 1 year minimum.

Terms Volunteers receive salary, furnished accommodation, insurance and travel costs. 40 hour week.

Briefing Broad orientation given to volunteers in writing and during interview. Regular contact maintained throughout stay with debriefing on return.

When to apply Recruitment all year.

Publications Information leaflet; various publications in Danish.

DEPARTEMENT EVANGELIQUE FRANCAIS D'ACTION APOSTOLIQUE

Address 102 Boulevard Arago, 75014 Paris, France Tel 320 7095

Contact Responsable du Service des envoyes et Cooperation

Countries Africa: Benin, Burkina Faso, Cameroon, Central African Republic, Chad, Gabon, Ivory Coast, Lesotho, Madagascar, Mozambique, Niger, Reunion, Rwanda, Sierra Leone, Togo, Zaire, Zambia. Caribbean: Martinique. Europe: France, Italy, Switzerland. Pacific: New Caledonia, Tahiti.

Organisation Originally founded in 1822 as the Societe des Missions de Paris, DEFAP has been in existence since 1971. As a Protestant church organisation with links in France and overseas it aims to improve international relations by spreading the message of evangelism. Its services cover missionary and development work, training of volunteers, distribution of funds and information.

Opportunities The majority of posts are for teachers of technical/science subjects in secondary schools. There are also posts in the medical, theological and technical fields. Recruits 30-40 volunteers, mostly French, annually.

Personal qualities Applicants should be open-minded and committed to the cultural and spiritual ideals of the organisation.

Age 21+

Qualifications A degree or equivalent qualification plus two years work experience usually necessary. Fluent French essential; English useful in some cases.

Length of service 2 years minimum; generally 3-4 years.

Terms Accommodation, insurance, travel and living costs provided for volunteer and dependents. A small allowance is paid before departure and volunteers receive one month's paid leave per year spent abroad. 40 hour week, more in the case of medical workers.

Briefing Compulsory orientation courses arranged, with debriefing sessions on return.

When to apply Six months in advance.

Publications *Recherche de Personnel* six-monthly list of vacancies; *Journal des Missions* quarterly magazine with a bi-monthly supplement.

DIENST OVER GRENZEN

Address Service Abroad, PO Box 177, 3700 AD Zeist, The Netherlands
Tel 24884

Contact The Secretariat

Countries Mainly in Africa, with limited opportunities in Asia and Latin America.

Organisation Founded in 1962, a personnel recruiting agency serving as mediator rather than employer, working on behalf of churches, church-related organisations and governments in the Third World. When DOG receives a request for personnel, a decision whether to recruit is taken within the framework of DOG's own policies and priorities. An insight into whether the project concerned contributes to the improvement of the socio-economic situation of the underprivileged groups in the developing countries and as to the precise task of the development workers within these projects is involved. It keeps a register of volunteers qualified in different professions and the agencies abroad can submit requests for personnel.

Opportunities There are vacancies in the medical, technical, educational, administration, financial and community development fields. Personnel required include doctors, nurses, physiotherapists and analysts; construction, mechanical and agricultural engineers; teachers in science, agriculture, mechanics, technical and vocational subjects; and social workers.

Personal qualities Volunteers should possess flexibility, social ability and a positive attitude towards development.

Age 24+

Qualifications Volunteers should be qualified to MSc/BSc degree level or equivalent. Previous experience an advantage.
All nationalities considered. Knowledge of Dutch and French/English required.

Length of service 3 years minimum.

Terms There are no set rules for salaries and allowances.
The local salary should cover living expenses, housing, insurance and, if possible, travel costs. Interview expenses not provided.

Briefing Compulsory orientation course arranged by a joint institute of the Protestant Missions in the Netherlands.
Additional training such as language or professional courses can also be arranged. Advice and debriefing provided on return if necessary.

When to apply Recruitment all year.

Publications *Doggersbank* quarterly communication bulletin, published in Dutch; information leaflet.

DIRECT RELIEF INTERNATIONAL

Address Volunteer Medical Services Division, PO Box 30820, Santa Barbara, CA 93130-0820, USA Tel 687 3694

Contact The Assignment Liaison Officer

Countries Africa: Egypt, Rwanda, Sierra Leone, Zaire.
Asia: Bangladesh, India, Nepal. Caribbean: Dominican Republic, St Lucia.
Far East: Korea, Taiwan, Thailand.
Latin America: Belize, Bolivia, Brazil, Chile, Colombia, Ecuador,
El Salvador, Guatemala, Honduras, Mexico, Nicaragua, Panama, Peru.
Pacific: American Samoa, Philippines.
North America: Indian reservations in the USA.

Organisation A non-profit, non-political, non-sectarian organisation founded in 1948, dedicated to providing health care assistance to medically underserved areas of the world. Working in partnership with private individuals and organisations, it responds to requests from hospitals and health centres for medical goods and volunteer medical, dental and para-medical assistance, and provides emergency and disaster relief throughout the world. It is dedicated to strengthening the health care base of developing nations as an essential step in promoting their productivity and self-sufficiency.

Opportunities Through its Medical Services Program, DRI fills requests for trained medical professionals; most requests are for doctors, surgeons, occupational, physical and speech therapists, psychiatrists, dieticians, medical administrators, pharmacists, nurses, health educators and medical technicians.
There are also opportunities for third and fourth year medical and dental students. Recruits 75-100 volunteers annually.

Personal qualities Applicants should be committed to sharing their medical skills for clinical needs as well as teaching and training local health workers. They should be motivated and able to adjust to changing living and working conditions.

Age 18+

Qualifications Relevant qualifications required and, dependent on location, previous experience and command of the local language. All nationalities considered. **HVC**

Length of service Short-term: 1-12 months. Long-term: 1 year or more.

Terms Short-term: most locations provide board and lodging; travel paid by the volunteer. Long-term: some locations provide compensation, stipend or pocket money, travel costs and malpractice insurance coverage. Families welcome, depending on available accommodation. Church groups and other organisations in the USA may sponsor volunteers.

When to apply Recruitment all year.

Publications *What's up at DRI* newsletter.

EMMAUS INTERNATIONAL

Address PO Box 41, 94222 Charenton Le Pont Cedex, France
Tel 893 2950

Contact The Secretary General

Country France. Approx 60 communities but only a few accept young
foreign volunteers of both sexes.

Organisation Founded in 1949 Emmaus International aims to help through
action every man, society and nation to live, assert and fulfill itself with
equal dignity through communication and sharing, and by devotion
simultaneously to emergency or long-term aid, to fight against the causes
of suffering, poverty and injustice. Emmaus organises ragpicking
communities, summer youth camps, Friends of Emmaus groups, plus
others which, although not committed to community life, share their ideals
and aims. Their work emphasises the waste of the world's resources and
constitutes the main source of financial aid for each group's actions.

Opportunities Volunteers are needed to work and live in rag pickers
communities, which involves collecting, sorting and selling secondhand or
used items such as paper, clothes, furniture, household goods, ironware
and metals. These communities are are not only self-sufficient through
their work, but support social or development projects throughout the
world. The communities essentially receive men, whatever their age or
background, who have suffered misfortunes and are often destitute with
social, family or professional problems, who are lonely, looking for a
home, security, friendship and a reason to live. With this work they earn a
living and share their benefit with people who suffer more than
themselves.

Personal qualities Volunteers should share the aims and objectives of the
movement, and be conscious of their responsibilities in community life, at
work and in relation to the problems of injustice.

Age 18+

Qualifications No academic qualifications or experience required.
Knowledge of French essential. **HVC**

Length of service 1 month minimum; open-ended commitment.

Terms Accommodation and food provided. Pocket money approx FF70
per week and insurance sometimes provided, depending on the
community. No travel paid. 40 hour week.

When to apply Recruitment all year. Application should be made to the
independent communities and local groups, quoting age, profession,
reason for application, time and duration of intended stay, knowledge of
French and whether in possession of a driving licence. Addresses
available from headquarters.

Publications Newsletters, leaflets and books.

FRANCISCAN VOLUNTEER COMMUNITY

Address 109 North Dearborn Street, Room 404, Chicago, IL 60602, USA
Tel 782 9660

Contact The Executive Director

Country USA

Organisation Founded in 1981, a group of lay people united in faith who strive to make Christ present in the modern world. Work mainly in conjunction with the various ministries of the Franciscan Friars of the Sacred Heart Province, serving in metropolitan areas and rural locales in Illinois, Texas and Wisconsin.

Opportunities The Community operates centres in Chicago: the St Francis Center, a soup kitchen serving meals and distributing clothes; the Franciscan House of Joseph and Mary, housing overnight individuals; and the Poverello House, which provides temporary lodging and assistance to stranded women; in Texas: St Francis Village, a retirement community; and in Wisconsin: a skills centre for native American Indians. Volunteers help the poor and hungry, and the needs of the parish or mission dictate the type of work to be done, including food service, sizing and sorting clothes, teaching, homemaking, social work, mechanics, construction and craft skills.

Personal qualities Volunteers should be practicising Catholics with a desire to live more deeply the life of Christ through service to the poor and their environment.

Age 18+

Qualifications Relevant qualifications needed for skilled posts; applicants should preferably be high school graduates or equivalent. All nationalities considered.

Length of service 1 year minimum.

Terms Volunteers live, eat and pray as a community; in almost all cases a private sleeping area is provided. Transportation, insurance, food and monthly pocket money provided on an individual basis.

Briefing Three day orientation programme/retreat held in Chicago to allow volunteers time for prayer and reflection and to introduce them to the parish or mission where they will be working.

When to apply Recruitment all year.

Publications Information leaflets.

FRIENDS OF ISRAEL EDUCATIONAL TRUST

Address Bridge in Britain Scheme, 25 Lyndale Avenue, London NW2 2QB
Tel 01-435 6803

Contact The Director

Country Israel

Organisation Founded in 1976, the Trust aims to promote in the UK a knowledge of Israel and its people via talks, lectures, presentations and working visits to Israel.

Opportunities The scheme offers 12 school leavers the chance to spend time in Israel. The programme involves working on a kibbutz; participating in an archaeological dig run by the University of Tel Aviv; and teaching in high schools or working in youth centres as part of a community service programme in a development town. Participants have the opportunity to meet working professionals and academics in their chosen subject and to take part in seminars, organised tours and independent travel.

Personal qualities Volunteers should be open to new experiences and want to participate in the pioneering spirit of modern Israel. They should be prepared to undertake any tasks/challenges set.

Age 18+

Qualifications No experience necessary, but most applicants are A level students. British nationals only.

Length of service 5 months, February-August, spending 2 months on a kibbutz, 2 months on a community service programme, and 3 weeks on an archaeological dig.

Terms Travel, basic lodging, food in canteen or self-catering and basic insurance provided, plus back-up from specialists throughout the programme. Token amount of pocket money provided on the kibbutz. Approx 30 hour week.

Briefing Full debriefing given on return, with ongoing contact.

When to apply By 1 October. Applicants should explain in an essay of a minimum 400 words their reasons for wishing to visit Israel. Shortlisted candidates are interviewed.

Publications Information leaflets.

FRONTIER APOSTOLATE

Address Box 7000, College Road, Prince George, BC V2N 3Z2, Canada
Tel 964 4559

Contact The Secretary

Country Canada

Organisation Founded in 1956 to promote Catholic education in the Diocese of Prince George, a large area of forest, mountain and ranch land in central and northern British Columbia. Provides an opportunity to live, experience and build a spirit of Christian community.

Opportunities Voluntary work is available for teachers, student supervisors, accountants, secretaries, child care workers, kitchen staff, bus drivers and maintenance workers. The main area of work is the Christian education of young white and native Indian students. Volunteers are also needed at homes for handicapped children and recovering alcoholics; in chancery, parish and school offices; and as parish workers in catechitics, visitation and liturgy preparation.

Personal qualities Applicants must be able to get along with others, have maturity, endurance and be sure of their reasons for volunteering. They should aim to be apostolic through active daily participation in the witness of living and have an appreciation of spiritual values.

Age 21-60

Qualifications Qualifications needed depend on the position offered. Experience necessary, especially for secretaries and teachers, but not for student supervisors or child care workers.
Good physical and mental health essential. Applicants not of the Catholic faith will be considered if they are basically in agreement with the ideals and aims of the Apostolate. Married couples accepted. Applicants should preferably be Canadian, American, British or Irish.

Length of service 2 years, starting August.

Terms Accommodation in private rooms, living in houses with 2-6 volunteers, helping with household chores. Monthly allowance of $110 in the first year, slightly higher in subsequent years.
Food allowance $150 per month. Volunteers pay travel to Canada, but subsidy may be given; fare home at end of service. Accident insurance provided. Three weeks holiday for each year of service, but minimum service must be completed before volunteer becomes eligible. In summer those directly engaged in education may take six weeks unpaid holiday plus $250 in lieu of board.

Briefing One week orientation course at end of August, followed by local orientation. Annual and zone conferences organised for volunteers to meet, exchange ideas and reaffirm commitment.

When to apply All applicants personally interviewed by Apostolate representative during March/April.

Publication Information leaflet.

FRONTIERS FOUNDATION/OPERATION BEAVER

Address 2622 Danforth Avenue, Toronto, Ontario M4C 1L7, Canada
Tel 690 3930

Contact The Program Coordinator

Country Canada

Organisation Aims to aid in all aspects of community development by supporting the needs and goals of communities and participating thereby in the direct relief of poverty. It also encourages people from culturally diverse backgrounds to meet one another and work together voluntarily, recognising that the local community and the world community advance together with strength.
Operation Beaver is a programme based on the partnership of communities with volunteers from around the world, to provide better housing and living conditions in low income communities in Canada or technical skills in the Third World.

Opportunities Volunteers work on practical projects in cooperation with native and non-native peoples in the rural Canadian communities of British Columbia, Alberta, Northwest Territories, Ontario, Prince Edward Island and Labrador, in well-defined and community-led development programmes. They construct, renovate and sometimes design frame and log houses, band offices and schools, as well as individual projects such as a pig pen and farm fence, children's home, greenhouse, kiln for a sawmill, cooperative store, church and cooperative fish processing plant.

Personal qualities Applicants should have faith in the philosophy, practical work and achievements of the Foundation, and be prepared to sustain their involvement and support for it to function effectively.

Age 18-81

Qualifications Volunteers with construction skills or previous volunteer service preferred. Skills such as engineering, architecture, graphics, French translating and public relations are always welcome in the head office or in the field.

Length of service 2 months in July and August, which can then be extended for up to 18 months.

Terms Salary not provided initially, although volunteers electing for an extension may be paid a modest weekly living allowance.
Accommodation, food and local travel expenses provided, but not travel to Canada.

Briefing Orientation and follow-up sessions arranged during the first 2 months.

When to apply. Recruitment all year.

Publications Annual Report.

GAP ACTIVITY PROJECTS (GAP) LTD

Address 2 South Drive, Leighton Park School, Reading, Berkshire RG2 7DP

Contact The Company Secretary

Countries Europe: Belgium, Federal Republic of Germany, Italy, Spain. Latin America: Chile, Falkland Islands. North America: Canada, USA. Pacific: Australia, New Zealand. South Africa; India; Israel.

Organisation A charity founded in 1972 to give those with a year between leaving school and going on to further education or vocational training the opportunity to travel to another country and live and work among its people.

Opportunities The majority of volunteer placements are in schools, where the opportunities include being teacher's aide, laboratory technician, assistant matron; coaching on the games field and adventure training; and contributing to music, drama and art. There are also placements on farms and kibbutzim, in hospitals and children's homes, and sometimes in offices or banks. Recruits approx 250 volunteers annually.

Personal qualities Applicants should be reliable, possess initiative and intelligence and be prepared to work hard.

Age 18-19

Qualifications High academic grades and experience are not of prime importance but this and foreign language requirements varies according to placement. Applicants must be British nationals.

Length of service Most school placements are for 8/9 months; most others for 6 months. Some placements begin September/October, but the majority start January/February.

Terms Board and accommodation in a flat or as a paying guest, and £20 per week pocket money provided. Volunteers are responsible for their travel and insurance costs, but advice is given. 40 hour week. Placement fee £100-£250.

Briefing For some schemes participants receive briefing on their placement and country of destination at GAP headquarters. Volunteers are required to write a report about their placement. GAP are always prepared to give advice or help to returned volunteers and some are personally debriefed.

When to apply Apply by end April for autumn departure; mid September for New Year.

Publications *Filling the GAP* and *This is GAP* booklets giving details of the schemes and information on the organisation.

GERMAN LEPROSY RELIEF ASSOCIATION

Address Deutsches Aussatzigen-Hilfswerk eV, Dominikanerplatz 4, Postfach 348, 8700 Wurzburg 11, Federal Republic of Germany
Tel 50784

Contact The Personnel Manager

Countries Africa: Egypt, Ethiopia, Liberia, Malawi, Senegal, Sierra Leone, Sudan, Tanzania, Togo, Uganda.
Caribbean: Dominican Republic. Latin America: Argentina, Bolivia, Brazil, Colombia, Paraguay, Peru.

Organisation Founded in 1957 with the tasks of sponsoring and establishing institutions to combat leprosy; training, education and other means of rehabilitation for leprosy patients; public health education and publicity. The declared aim of the association is to integrate leprosy control services into general health care programmes wherever possible, as well as supporting public health care work and training of local personnel for the medical and social welfare sector.

Opportunities There are vacancies for skilled long-term volunteers, helping at treatment and training centres, on national health care and control programmes, and in the general care of leprosy patients.

Personal qualities Applicants must have a commitment to the care of leprosy.

Age 25+

Qualifications Academic qualifications required together with several years skilled, professional experience. All nationalities considered. Knowledge of English, Spanish and French required depending on the host country.

Length of service 3 years.

Terms Accommodation in house or apartment, monthly allowance depending on marital status, insurance and travel provided.
40-50 hour week.

Briefing Compulsory orientation course arranged. Assistance provided for returned volunteers to enable them to reintegrate.

When to apply Recruitment all year.

Publications Information leaflets; several publications in the German language.

THE GIRL GUIDES ASSOCIATION (UK)

Address 17-19 Buckingham Palace Road, London SW1W OPT
Tel 01-834 6242

Contact The International Secretary

Countries India; Mexico; Switzerland.

Organisation Founded in 1910, the Association aims to provide a programme embracing a wide range of leisure-time activities and interests which, while enjoyable in themselves, have an underlying educational purpose, namely, to develop individual character based on the values expressed in the Promise and Law.

Opportunities Volunteer work is available overseas at centres owned by the World Association of Girl Guides and Girl Scouts. Projects may include assisting the development of Guide Associations in other countries, training adult leaders or administration duties in connection with Guide Houses. The work is sometimes strenuous and the hours long.

Personal qualities These are determined by the Guider-in-Charge for each centre.

Age 18+

Qualifications Qualifications and experience required vary according to the position. Volunteers must be members of the Association. **HVC**

Length of service Variable

Terms Board, accommodation and pocket money provision vary according to the position. Insurance provided in some cases. Travel costs usually paid by the volunteer. Advice is given to participants on obtaining sponsorship. Members are encouraged to write articles for the magazines on their return.

When to apply Recruitment all year.

Publications *The Brownie*; *Today's Guide*; *Guiding* magazines.

GREEN DESERTS LTD

Address Rougham, Bury St Edmunds, Suffolk IP30 9LY Tel Beyton 70265

Contact The Company Secretary

Country Sudan

Organisation According to a recent United Nations Environment Programme survey, one third of the surface of the earth is in danger of turning to desert and 470 million people living there, over 1 in 10 of the world's population, are now starving. A charity founded in 1976, Green Deserts believes that it is possible to halt the desertification process and reclaim the areas lost to useful production, bringing permanent relief from famine. Their operation channels resources into community forestry, agriculture and appropriate technology, with the aim of enabling rural communities to become self-reliant.

Opportunities A limited number of skilled volunteers are needed. Projects include planting goat-resistant trees and building simple rain catchments to establish a system of sustainable forestry in the Sahara's southern fringe; encouraging the regeneration of shelter belt trees in the desert by the Nile; building percolation dams to retain flash flood waters long enough for trees to be planted and survive in the wadis in remote mountainous areas. Village tree nurseries and mobile teams are planned for the future.

Personal qualities Applicants should demonstrate a sincere desire to pass on their skills and a general level of acceptance of other people's lifestyles and customs.

Age 18+

Qualifications Relevant qualifications and experience essential; knowledge of local languages useful. All nationalities considered.

Length of service 2 years, beginning September/October.

Terms Dependent on the level of funding for the project, volunteers are expected to find some or all of their travel, insurance and station allowance costs. Advice given to participants on obtaining sponsorship. 35-40 hour week.

Briefing Compulsory orientation course. Resettlement and debriefing service provided on return.

When to apply Apply by July/August at the latest.

Publications *Green Deserts* regular magazine.

HABITAT FOR HUMANITY INC

Address 419 W Church Street, Americus, GA 31709, USA Tel 924 6935

Contact The Director of Volunteer Services

Countries Africa: Kenya, Uganda, Zaire, Zambia.
Latin America: Bolivia, Guatemala, Nicaragua, Peru.
Haiti; India; Papua New Guinea; USA.

Organisation An ecumenical Christian housing ministry which aims to provide a decent house in a decent community for God's people in need. This is accomplished by building low-cost homes for sale to poor families at no profit and no interest on a 20 year mortgage. Currently they are building houses in 11 Third World countries and 64 communities in the USA.

Opportunities Volunteers are needed with construction skills such as carpentry and masonry; office skills such as typing and book keeping; and administrative skills such as fundraising and public relations. Recruits over 100 volunteers annually.

Personal qualities Applicants should have a strong desire to house the homeless. Although it is an ecumenical ministry, making no demands on denominational affiliation, applicants should have a Christian commitment.

Age 18+

Qualifications No academic qualifications necessary, but relevant skills required. Experience not always needed. All nationalities considered.
HVC

Length of service 3 years minimum service in the Third World; negotiable long and short-term service in USA.

Terms Projects in the Third World: housing, insurance and language tuition provided and, depending on the project, pocket money. Volunteers are asked to raise $300 per month stipend and as much of their travel costs as possible, before they go.

Projects in USA: housing and utilities provided, plus a small weekly food stipend; volunteers meet their travel and insurance costs.

Advice given to all participants on obtaining sponsorship through denominational agencies, churches and other sources.

Briefing Compulsory 3 month orientation course arranged.
Returned volunteers receive a short debriefing programme.

When to apply Recruitment all year.

Publications *Habitat Happenings* monthly newsletter; *Habitat World* quarterly newspaper; plus books by the founder, a collection of essays on its work, and film/slide shows.

HELP THE AGED

Address St James's Walk, London EC1R OBE Tel 01-253 0253

Contact The Personnel Officer

Country Africa

Organisation Founded in 1961, a national charity dedicated to improving the quality of life of the elderly in the UK and overseas and in alleviating distress caused by poverty, sickness, bad housing, loneliness, natural disaster, political upheaval, ageism and discrimination. Fundamental to the work is the belief that the world's aged should be able to live full lives as integrated members of society. Overseas priorities include the fight against urban destitution, supporting health care programmes focusing on clean water provision, advising governments on social policy for the elderly and providing emergency supplies. Primarily a funding rather than an operational agency; financial support is given to self-help projects in over 60 countries.

Opportunities Doctors and nurses are recruited from time to time to work in contexts where a lack of medical skills is a serious constraint to development or an obstacle to immediate emergency relief. Recently this has included primary health care campaigns in rural areas, such as an eye-care team in Somalia and a refugee health team in the Sudan. Occasionally there are places for administrators or technicians. Recruits 20 volunteers annually.

Personal qualities Applicants should have good communication skills, the ability to live and work as a team, plus a commitment to the cause of justice in the developing countries.

Age 25+

Qualifications Relevant qualifications required. Good UK experience necessary; overseas experience preferred and essential for SENs. It is an absolute requirement that participants have the right of entry to the UK. Fluent English essential. **HVC**

Length of service 6 months initially; longer for projects in long-term community development.

Terms Accommodation, usually on site in team compound or house, insurance, travel and small salary provided. Other allowances for equipment and leave sometimes arranged. Hours worked vary, but emergency relief in particular can involve a 7 day week shift system.

Briefing Compulsory briefing and personnel formalities arranged at the London office. Returned volunteers are encouraged to discuss projects informally.

When to apply Recruitment all year.

Publications Annual Report; *Africa Report*; a wide range of books and audio visual material from the Education Department.

INDIAN VOLUNTEERS FOR COMMUNITY SERVICE

Address 36 Headstone Road, Harrow HA1 2PE Tel 01-863 9544

Contact The General Secretary

Country India

Organisation A registered charity founded in 1981 which involves young people in community service, providing them with the opportunity to discover and understand the culture of their origin, and enabling them to perceive the causes of conflict and disparity in society. Organises an advisory and resource service and courses on the issues of development and international interdependence, especially in the context of the relationship between the Indian subcontinent and Britain.

Opportunities Volunteers work in rural development projects usually in three categories: helping with children in a school or nursery; working with small-scale agricultural machinery, driving and maintaining tractors, and surveying; and office work, including correspondence, typing, compiling newsletters and formulating applications. Also opportunities in local communities working with children, women, the elderly and disabled; and teaching English as a second language. The work involves living and working with people who respond positively to human values and volunteers will be involving themselves in the lives and problems of the community, facing new challenges and experiences and developing social skills and responsibilities.

Personal qualities Applicants should have imagination and commonsense, a readiness to learn and an understanding of their role, to benefit from this cultural and educational experience.
They must love people, care and have compassion for the community, and be prepared to work hard at anything to improve the quality of life.

Age 18+

Qualifications No qualifications or experience necessary.
Some experience needed for operating agricultural machinery.
Any nationality may apply, but volunteers must be of Asian origin.

Length of service 6 months minimum, normally leaving September-December, and returning March-June.

Terms Basic accommodation, which may be shared, and food provided in the village. Participants pay all travel costs and personal expenses. Pocket money and insurance sometimes provided if volunteer is under 25 and eligible for a Silver Jubilee Trust grant. Advice given on obtaining sponsorship.

Briefing Compulsory orientation course organised. Meetings with committee members and other returned volunteers, participation in activities plus the orientation of new volunteers organised as an advice/debriefing service. Membership fee £5.

When to apply Recruitment all year.

Publications Quarterly newsletter; Annual Report; leaflets.

INNISFREE VILLAGE

Address Route 2, Box 506, Crozet, VA 22932, USA Tel 823 5400

Contact The Director

Country USA

Organisation Innisfree's goal is to provide a lifetime residential facility for people with mental handicap. The staff consists entirely of volunteers who live and work together with mentally handicapped co-workers in a natural and humanistic environment.

Opportunities Acting as houseparents and co-workers, volunteers are needed to work on the 400 acre farm in the foothills of the Blue Ridge Mountains with the choice of working in the bakery, weavery, woodshop, garden, free school or village store. Volunteers living in Charlottesville work in the pottery. Recruits 18 volunteers annually.

Personal qualities Volunteers need energy, enthusiasm, patience and a willingness to work with the 'differently-abled'. They must be interested in the community process in a very rural setting and in excellent health.

Age 21+

Qualifications Volunteers must be high school graduates or equivalent. Some experience with mentally retarded, recently brain injured or emotionally ill people preferred. Craft skills greatly appreciated. All nationalities considered. Fluent English essential.

Length of service Volunteers are sponsored under the International Exchange Visitors Programme for 1 year only.

Terms Volunteers have their own room in a house of 2-11 people, and each house has a food allowance. $120 per month spending money, $20 per day for vacations, $100 bonus at Christmas, medical insurance and up to $250 for dental expenses, provided. Travel costs are paid by the volunteer. Volunteers work up to 24 hours per day, 5 days per week. Two consecutive days free per week and annual holiday entitlement of 21 days.

Briefing The first month is a mandatory trial period with four orientation sessions covering a brief history of the village and its guidelines and volunteers are encouraged to get to know the village as well as possible before settling down in one house. At the end of this period, the community evaluates and decides the best placement for the volunteer.

When to apply Recruitment all year.

THE INSTITUTE OF CULTURAL AFFAIRS

Address 277 St Ann's Road, London N15 5RG Tel 01-802 2848

Contact The Volunteer Service Programme Training Officer

Countries Africa: Egypt, Ivory Coast, Kenya, Zambia.
Asia: India. Caribbean: Jamaica.
Europe: Austria, Belgium, Federal Republic of Germany, Portugal, Spain.
Far East: Hong Kong, Japan, Taiwan.
Latin America: Brazil, Guatemala, Peru, Venezuela.

Organisation Founded in the UK in 1968 as a registered charity, a research, training and demonstration organisation concerned with the human factor in development. The Institute promotes methods which enhance the self-reliance of local communities and through its Volunteer Service Programme offers opportunities for involvement in a wide range of community development schemes and development education. Development is seen not as a cluster of benefits 'given' to people in need, but rather a process by which a populace acquires greater mastery over its own destiny.

Opportunities Volunteers are needed in four main areas. In Village Cluster Development volunteers work as part of a team spreading the concept of self-help, which has led to the initiation of economic schemes such as community bakeries, farm irrigation, literacy, health and education projects. Support Centres coordinate activities for various aspects of development work including office organisation, fundraising, translation, report writing and publicity. Through Lifestyle Demonstration, developing community life, discovering new vocational challenges, appropriate alternatives for the future are explored and skills are needed in energy, health, viable economics and linking groups with similar interests. Special Projects Development includes research and evaluation, designing development education programmes, teaching adults basic skills, small business apprenticeship schemes, coordination of the Volunteers Service Programme and worldwide information exchange. Recruits 65-80 volunteers annually, 15-20 for work in Europe.

Personal qualities Applicants should have commonsense and adaptability, and be mature enough to cope creatively with the complex situations that occur in serious community and development efforts.

Age 17-70

Qualifications Relevant expertise in the fields of economic and social development a distinct advantage. Previous experience not always necessary. All nationalities considered. Previous knowledge of languages required for work in Europe.

Length of service Europe: 3 months minimum, 9 months preferred. Third World: 9 months minimum, 12 months preferred.

Terms Volunteers live and work as part of a team in basic rural and urban settings, under conditions similar to the local population. Long hours, six days per week. They are responsible for their own funding, including travel, board and lodging, pocket money and preparation costs in London; these costs depend upon length of stay and destination but are

continued overleaf

usually within the range £1100-£1800. Advice and encouragement given on obtaining sponsorship.

Briefing Orientation weekends and interviews followed by a compulsory preparation and orientation month in London. Language study arranged for volunteers going to the Third World. Returned volunteers are encouraged to write a report and are hosted at the Institute for two days to report on their experiences.

When to apply Recruitment all year.

Publications Information leaflets and newsletters.

INTERCULTURAL EDUCATIONAL PROGRAMMES

Address Seymour Mews House, Seymour Mews, London W1H 9PE
Tel 01-486 5462

Contact The Programme Administrator

Countries People's Republic of China; Ghana; Sri Lanka.

Organisation Founded in 1947 as the American Field Service, AFS International/Intercultural Programs now operate in the UK as IEP. An international voluntary organisation providing educational opportunities to learn about other cultures through first hand experience and, through a variety of exchange programmes, aims to promote peace and international understanding. There are limited opportunities for teachers to work overseas on a voluntary basis.

Opportunities Qualified teachers of appropriate subjects are needed in secondary schools teaching science, agricultural science or mathematics; to teach English as a Foreign Language to trainee teachers; and in teacher training colleges in Africa.

Personal qualities Volunteers provide a professional service in countries where there is a real need, but they are also learning on a very personal level about the cultural values of the host country; teachers are placed in host family accommodation and provided with a thorough orientation programme. All volunteers are expected to use their experience to promote intercultural learning on their return.

Qualifications Applicants should be qualified teachers, preferably with at least 2-3 years experience. PGCE, BEd or equivalent qualifications required in appropriate subjects. TEFL qualification desirable for Sri Lanka and China. Applicants for China should also have completed at least one year's study of Mandarin; they will be teaching part-time and studying for the remainder.

Length of service 6-7 months in China, starting in January; otherwise 1 year with option for a second year, starting September.

Terms University accommodation in China; self-catering accommodation during term, with host families during vacations in Ghana; host family accommodation in Sri Lanka. Local salary or allowances paid to cover living expenses. Insurance and travel provided. Application fee £5, plus for China a participation fee.

Briefing Compulsory orientation course provided before departure and, in Ghana and Sri Lanka, on arrival. AFS offices also provide advice and support throughout the year. Returned volunteers are provided with informal evaluation and a small resettlement allowance; they are also expected to become involved in the organisation, helping with orientation and fundraising for future participants.

When to apply As early as possible.

Publications Annual Report; *Teacher Programme Newsletter*.

INTERNATIONAL LIAISON

Address US Catholic Coordinating Center for Lay Missioners, 1234 Massachusetts Avenue, NW, Washington, DC 20005, USA Tel 638 4197

Contact The Communications Coordinator

Countries USA; Third World, majority of American volunteers.

Organisation Founded in 1963, the Catholic Church's official centre for promotion, referral and recruitment of lay volunteer missioners through a network of 115 mission-sending and receiving agencies. Although Catholic in orientation, it functions interdenominationally and in no way limits itself to strictly Catholic contacts or concerns. Its prime function is carried out through the facilities of the US Catholic dioceses and religious communities who sponsor and conduct lay volunteer programmes. A link is provided between interested lay individuals with expertise and organisations best able to utilise their skills, and IL also acts as an information and advice service.

Opportunities Volunteers are needed to work on a wide range of projects; over 100 professions are listed in the directory of lay mission opportunities, from accountants through carpenters, farmers, journalists, nurses, pilots, teachers to welders.
Recruits over 900 volunteers annually for the USA alone.

Personal qualities Applicants should have a genuine desire to serve humanity and God through service to those in need, a level of maturity indicative of the ability to adapt to mission conditions, open mindedness to change and to other cultures, and stability of purpose.

Age Varies according to the agency.

Qualifications High school education or equivalent required by most programmes. Relevant qualifications necessary in many cases for medical and educational placements. Most projects recruiting professional volunteers require experience in the chosen field. All nationalities considered. **HVC**

Length of service 1 or 2 years, usually starting late summer/September.

Terms Most programmes provide room and board or food allowance, stipend, medical insurance and travel to and from the mission site. 40 hour week. Many agency members will assist with sponsorship.

Briefing Orientation courses provided if appropriate.
Reorientation programmes vary from group to group, but a programme for returned missioners is encouraged.

When to apply Recruitment all year.

Publications *The Response* a directory of lay mission opportunities; *Lay Mission* quarterly newsletter; *Summer and Short-term Programmes*. *Christians in Mission* essays on formation and operation of lay programmes.

INTERNATIONAL VOLUNTARY SERVICE

Address Ceresole House, 53 Regent Road, Leicester LE1 6YL
Tel'Leicester 541862

In Ireland: Voluntary Service International, PO Box 652, 95 Merrion
Square, Dublin 2 Tel Dublin 685681

Contact The Selection and Recruitment Officer

Countries Africa: Botswana, Lesotho, Mozambique, Swaziland, West
Africa. Also a few opportunities in Asia.

Organisation Founded in 1931, IVS is the UK branch of Service Civil
International, a movement started in the 1920s for the promotion of peace.
It exists to provide opportunities for men and women, young and old,
irrespective of their race, nationality, creed or politics, to join together in
giving useful voluntary service to the community in a spirit of friendship
and international understanding. **BVP**

Opportunities Skilled volunteers are needed to work on a variety of
agricultural, medical, educational, technical and administrative projects.
IVS have received most requests for agriculturalists, agricultural
engineers, farm managers, horticulturalists; midwives, nurse tutors,
doctors, dentists, laboratory technicians; science and maths teachers,
adult and non-formal education specialists, handicraft trainers; builders,
carpenters/joiners, civil engineers, architects/planners, water engineers,
mechanics; small enterprise managers and accountants. Recruits approx
35 volunteers annually. IVS also recruit short-term volunteers for
international workcamps; see *Working Holidays*.

Personal qualities Applicants should want to work in a spirit of equality
with people who are trying to free themselves from all aspects of
underdevelopment, including poverty, ill-health and economic, social and
educational deprivation. They should have a commitment to cooperating
with others across boundaries of race, class, sex and religion, and a
desire to share and pass on skills without personal financial gain.

Age 21-70

Qualifications Qualifications in a relevant recognised skill or discipline
usually required although sometimes substantial experience is accepted;
manual skills are as relevant as professional qualifications. Experience in
voluntary or community work an advantage; evidence of ability to learn
languages desirable. Applicants must be resident in the UK or Ireland.
Couples without dependent children are welcome, provided both
partners have skills or qualifications acceptable to the programme and
can be posted together. **HVC**

Length of service 2 years minimum.

Terms Simple accommodation provided plus a modest living allowance
which varies from country to country. Return air travel, insurance cover,
kit and equipment allowance, resettlement grant and National Insurance
contributions provided. Volunteers are encouraged to raise funds and
advice is given on obtaining sponsorship.

continued overleaf

Briefing Selection weekends are held and successful candidates take part in a compulsory training programme including orientation, workcamp participation, home study, specialist skills adaptation, country briefing and language courses.
Returned volunteers receive a dossier giving advice on resettlement; they are a valuable resource and are encouraged to participate in IVS UK activities, in particular, the selection, recruitment and training of volunteers.

When to apply Recruitment all year.

Publications *Service* newsletter; information leaflets.

INTERNATIONAL VOLUNTARY SERVICES INC

Address 1424-16th Street, NW, Suite 504, Washington, DC 20036, USA
Tel 387 5533

Contact The Recruitment Officer

Countries Africa: Sudan, Zimbabwe. Asia: Bangladesh.
Caribbean: Antigua, Dominica, Nevis, St Lucia, St Vincent.
Latin America: Bolivia, Ecuador.

Organisation Founded in 1953, a private, independent, non-profit,
technical assistance agency working in small scale rural development
projects with local organisations. It places volunteers providing expertise
which would otherwise be unavailable and seeks to transfer skills in order
to enable the poor to be more self-reliant, strengthening them to help
themselves through collective action.

Opportunities Through local organisations there are vacancies in the
fields of agriculture, food production, small business/cooperative
development, health care and training, nutrition, engineering,
intermediate technology and community development. With the help of
volunteers, indigenous groups have become increasingly effective in
responding to a variety of needs.

Personal qualities Applicants must have a desire to work with local
organisations and people, and to contribute to their efforts to become
more self-reliant.

Qualifications Volunteers must be graduates with a minimum of two
years practical work experience. Previous experience in overseas rural
development or in a cross-cultural setting preferred. All nationalities
considered. Volunteers must have a knowledge of Spanish for Latin
America, and the ability to learn a local language in other countries. A
large percentage of personnel are recruited from outside the USA,
reflecting the commitment to make the organisation more international.

Length of service 2-3 years.

Terms Furnished housing with utilities, a monthly cost of living allowance
to cover food and other necessities, group health and life insurance, travel
and US$200 allowance provided.

Briefing Short Washington orientation course sometimes precedes a
longer compulsory orientation in the country of assignment.

When to apply Recruitment all year.

Publications Annual Report; information literature.

THE JINJA GROUPS TRUST

Address 1 Hillsleigh Road, London W8 7LE Tel 01-727 5143

Contact The Chairman

Countries Dominica; India.

Organisation Founded in 1968, a charitable trust set up to enable young people to make a useful contribution in the developing world. Through the use of practical skills volunteers work on a variety of community development projects, encouraging local communities to help themselves. Jinja volunteers gain a unique understanding of the developing world and bring home a valuable insight into other cultures which can be used to foster greater understanding between peoples.

Opportunities Village projects need a limited number of skilled volunteers including irrigation and construction engineers, carpenters, agricultural, medical and crafts instructors, teachers and nurses.

Personal qualities Applicants should possess a basic Christian motivation and a willingness to work hard, often in difficult conditions.

Age 18-25

Qualifications Volunteers must have a high level of qualification with experience in one or more practical skills and, if necessary, be prepared to undertake voluntary part-time further training. British nationals only.

Length of service 2 years minimum.

Terms Volunteers receive bed and board at local standard, a small amount of pocket money, fares, insurance and National Insurance contributions. Encouragement and advice is given on raising sponsorship.

Briefing Compulsory orientation course arranged. Returned volunteers are encouraged to play an active part in Jinja support activities.

When to apply Volunteers are recruited as projects arise and the waiting period may be considerable before a particular skill is required.

Publications Newsletter; information leaflets.

JONGEREN VRIJWILLIGERS CORPS

Address Willem Witsenplein 2, 2596 BK The Hague, Netherlands
Tel 245008

Contact The Secretary General

Countries Africa; some opportunities in Asia and Latin America.

Organisation Founded in 1962 an umbrella organisation for Dutch non-governmental organisations involved in sending skilled, experienced long-term development workers to the Third World. It coordinates activities concerned with sending and co-financing development workers, and acts as a platform for the exchange of information between the organisations.

Opportunities Assignments are offered in the medical, technical, agricultural and formal/informal education sectors.

Personal qualities Applicants should have an awareness of the problems of injustice and the unequal distribution of wealth, power and opportunities abroad and at home; solidarity with underprivileged people; and an open mind to learn from people in Third World countries.

Age 25+

Qualifications Volunteers should be graduates or have higher professional qualifications. Knowledge of languages needed depending on the host country. **HVC**

Length of service 3-4 years minimum.

Terms The type of board and accommodation depends on the host organisation. Local salary rate, insurance and travel provided.

Briefing Compulsory orientation course organised. Debriefing interview and weekends arranged for returned volunteers.

When to apply Recruitment all year.

Publications Annual reports in Dutch.

LALMBA ASSOCIATION

Address 7685 Quartz Street, Golden, CO 80403, USA Tel 420 1810

Contact The Medical Director

Countries Africa: Kenya, Sudan.

Organisation A non-profit organisation defining itself as the world's smallest international relief agency; the word lalmba means place of hope. Its aims are to provide adequate health care and to teach the local population to care for their health needs. Work was started in 1962 in Ethiopia and moved to the Nubian desert on the borders of Sudan and Ethiopia with the increase of refugees during the late 1970s. Mobile clinics serve patients in the UN-sponsored refugee camps as well as the nomadic groups of the area; those in need of more intense medical treatment are taken to the Lalmba Medical Unit in Showak. The Association has responded to the famine emergency by creating a Special Forces Medical Unit; other projects include a food distribution and nutrition programme; a prosthetic clinic; eye clinics; and an orphanage.

Opportunities The main requirements are for doctors, surgeons and nurses. Physicians are responsible for teaching and supervising native community health workers, general medical practice, and providing primary health care with preventive medicine and education. Nurses have an expanded role and their work includes physical examinations, internal lab studies and diagnosis. Staff travel to the refugee camps and villages, providing medication for malnutrition and ailments such as dysentery, parasites, malaria, tuberculosis, meningitis and eye disease.

Personal qualities Applicants must have dedication and be committed to serving extremely poor, famine-stricken refugees.

Age 25+

Qualifications Relevant medical qualifications and experience essential. All nationalities considered. Good command of English required.

Length of service 1-2 years; short-term positions occasionally available.

Terms Accommodation provided in well-appointed grass huts, with electricity and water nearby, and communal catering.
Positions are non-salaried; all living expenses, insurance and needed materials are provided. Travel costs are met for long-term positions; advice on sponsorship given to those who have to find their travel costs. Eight hour day, five day week.

Briefing Lalmba meet and brief all volunteers personally; orientation organised in the form of videos and slides.

When to apply Recruitment all year.

Publications Newsletter; information leaflets.

LANKA JATIKA SARVODAYA SHRAMADANA SANGAMAYA

Address Damsak Mandira, 98 Rawatawatte Road, Moratuwa, Sri Lanka
Tel 7159

Contact The Executive Director

Country Sri Lanka

Organisation Founded in 1958, the movement is a large, non-governmental people's self-development effort covering nearly 6000 villages. These rural people have provided a practical possibility of realising Mahatma Gandhi's concept of a world society where the well-being of all shall be ensured. It aims to create awareness among economically and socially deprived communities and to mobilise latent human and material potential for the satisfaction of basic human needs in a manner that ensures sustainable development, and to develop strategies and implement action programmes for this concept.

Opportunities Volunteers are needed mainly on village-level development projects in agriculture, animal husbandry, agriculture-based industry, appropriate technology, irrigation, sanitation, house construction, energy conservation and the development of alternative energy sources. Opportunities also exist for teachers in pre-school and primary education, and for the provision of preventive and curative health care including nursing, first aid, nutrition and feeding programmes, health education and rehabilitation of the handicapped.

Personal qualities A willingness to teach and to learn is the main consideration; applicants should have an awareness of their responsibility to improve human conditions wherever needed and able to work in sometimes difficult circumstances. They should also have a commitment to the promotion of peace and international understanding, and to an ideal that leads to the equitable distribution of the world's resources according to need.

Age 18+

Qualifications Skills and experience vouched for by a recognised organisation or individual preferred, but specialised skills are not a priority requirement and academic qualifications are optional. All nationalities considered.

Length of service 6 months minimum.

Terms Board and lodging provided at a cost not exceeding Rs165 per day, but may be less in outstations. Volunteers are expected to meet their own travel, insurance and living expenses.
A leaflet is available giving guidelines on obtaining sponsorship.

Briefing Compulsory orientation course organised. End of service evaluation provided, at which the volunteer's subsequent activities and placement in the home country is discussed.

When to apply Recruitment all year.

Publications Various pamphlets on the work and ideals of the movement.

LAY VOLUNTEERS INTERNATIONAL ASSOCIATION

Address Corso IV Novembre 28, 12100 Cuneo, Italy Tel 62558

Contact The General Secretary

Countries Africa: Burkina Faso, Burundi, Cameroon, Ethiopia, Gambia, Guinea-Bissau, Kenya, Mali, Senegal.

Organisation Founded in 1967 with the dual aim of promoting Christianity and economic development in the Third World. It believes that a revival in Third World countries can only take place if they produce the goods they need and the industrialised nations pay a fair price for the products. Through the activities of its volunteers the Association works for a more fraternal way of life based on solidarity, justice and communion.

Opportunities Doctors, nurses and nutritionists are needed to train nurses and auxiliary medical staff, run mobile vaccination clinics, initiate nutrition, family planning, hygiene and first aid information campaigns, and assist in the provision of primary health care. Agricultural specialists are needed in animal husbandry, food production and marketing, reafforestation and farmer training. Technical instructors are needed for carpentry, housing, cooking, needlework and the production of construction materials. The Association also makes special use of experts in water provision, particularly the construction of wells, water pans, aquaducts, canals and irrigation projects.

Personal qualities Christian motivation, dedication, hard work and adaptability required.

Age 20/22+

Qualifications Qualifications needed vary depending on the assignment. Professional experience necessary. All nationalities considered. Knowledge of English and/or French required. **HVC**

Length of service 30 months

Terms Volunteers receive board and lodging, travel and insurance, and the equivalent of £50 pocket money per month.

Briefing Compulsory orientation course arranged.

When to apply Recruitment all year.

Publications *Notiziario Volontari* monthly magazine.

THE MEDICAL MISSIONARY ASSOCIATION

Address 6 Canonbury Place, London N1 2NJ Tel 01-359 1313

Contact The Secretary

Countries Worldwide

Organisation Founded in 1878 the Association works in cooperation with missionary societies to help further the cause of medical missions. It administers the OYSTER - One Year's Service To Encourage Recruiting - Scheme for doctors, and holds a large stock of reference material and information, and organises seminars and annual exhibitions.

Opportunities The Oyster Scheme provides grants enabling young Christian doctors to serve in mission hospitals, making a useful contribution to the work of the hospitals and providing stimulus and encouragement to the existing medical staff. After the scheme, participants are encouraged to apply for full missionary service.

Personal qualities Applicants must be practising Christians and willing to be guided by those in authority in their assigned hospitals.

Age 24+

Qualifications Applicants must be registered medical practitioners and single citizens of the UK or Ireland.

Length of service 1 year; can be extended to 2 years.

Terms Accommodation, insurance, normal missionary allowance and return air fare provided.

Briefing Seminars arranged.

When to apply Applications must be made in good time to the grant committee which meets in January, April, July and October.

Publications Two books: *Saving Health*; *Simple Dental Care for Rural Hospitals*; information leaflets.

METHODIST CHURCH OVERSEAS DIVISION

Address 25 Marylebone Road, London NW1 5JR Tel 01-935 2541

Contact The Secretary for Overseas Service

Countries Africa: Cameroon, Ghana, Ivory Coast, Kenya, Sierra Leone, Zambia, Zimbabwe.
Asia: Bangladesh, India, Nepal.
Far East: Indonesia, Japan, Korea, Malaysia, Singapore.
Pacific: Fiji, Papua New Guinea, Solomon Islands, Tonga, Western Samoa.

Organisation Founded in 1786, the section of the Methodist Church which conducts its relationship with overseas churches; part of that relationship means sometimes recruiting suitably qualified workers to share in the world of the Church there.
Also keeps the Church in the UK informed and the relationship alive.

Opportunities Types of voluntary work include posts for ministers, theological educators, teachers, doctors, nurses/midwives, agriculturalists, administrators and occasionally, engineers.

Personal qualities Applicants must have a commitment to Christ, want to share in the life and work of another church and a God-given sense of call and adventure. They should also be flexible, adaptable, with imagination and a sense of humour.

Age 23+

Qualifications Suitable qualifications, relevant expertise and experience necessary. Applicants must reside in the UK.

Length of service 3 years minimum.

Terms Self-catering furnished accommodation, stipend/allowance, National Insurance contributions and travel provided.

Briefing Language training given if necessary. Orientation course arranged and, on return, debriefing interview and course for volunteers to reflect on their experiences and look forward.

When to apply Recruitment all year.

Publications Regular vacancy lists; leaflets.

MISSION AVIATION FELLOWSHIP

Address Ingles Manor, Castle Hill Avenue, Folkestone, Kent CT20 2TN

Contact The Personnel Manager

Countries Africa: Cameroon, Central African Republic, Chad, Ethiopia, Kenya, Lesotho, Mozambique, Tanzania, Zaire, Zimbabwe.

Organisation A Christian organisation founded in 1947 and committed to helping the church in isolated areas by providing aircraft, pilots and the back-up that air transport work of this nature demands. The Fellowship helps to spread the Gospel, life and hope in spiritual and physical terms to thousands of people, providing an essential service to national pastors, church leaders, missionaries and medical and relief agency personnel, flying them to places where they are needed most. They also transport food, equipment, medical and agricultural supplies, emergency relief and other essential materials to remote and otherwise inaccessible locations, and are on call as an aerial ambulance service.

Opportunities A limited number of volunteers are needed for aircraft maintenance work to the highest safety standards, building work and occasionally administration. Volunteers work in partnership with Christian organisations, forming a unifying link between individuals or families working at lonely outposts.

Personal qualities Volunteers should have a Christian commitment, be active in the life of the church, and have a gift for technical service. Staff are selected for their skill, temperament and spiritual maturity.

Age 18+

Qualifications Previous experience of aircraft maintenance essential; engineers must hold appropriate professional licences.
Applications from suitably qualified couples accepted. All nationalities considered.

Length of service 2-3 months minimum.

Terms Accommodation with a family, 'workman's compensation' insurance and travel from main centres to rural bases provided. Volunteers provide their own air fares and pocket money. 40 hour week.

Briefing Short period of orientation organised at the office, and all personnel are given special training before they become active in the field. Guidance for the future is given in preparation for the return home.

When to apply Volunteers can apply at any time, but the summer months are preferable.

Publications *MAF News* quarterly magazine.

THE MISSIONS TO SEAMEN

Address St Michael Paternoster Royal, College Hill, London EC4R 2RL
Tel 01-248 5202

Contact The Secretary to The Assistant General Secretary

Countries At some 20 seaports around the world, particularly in developing countries: Africa, Asia, Australia, Caribbean, Europe, Far East, Latin and North America.

Organisation An Anglican missionary society founded in 1856, caring for the spiritual, material and moral welfare of seafarers around the globe. The Missions help to combat isolation, exploitation and the dangers of the sea, working for improvements in conditions, education and welfare, serving seafarers of every race, colour and creed, offering a ministry of word, sacrament, counselling care and Christian welcome. The most important feature is the visit of the chaplain and staff to each ship on arrival in port.

Opportunities There are volunteer service schemes for student assistants, providing an opportunity to be involved in practical Christian service within the shipping industry. Work is varied and involves visiting ships, conducting sightseeing tours, arranging sporting events, visiting hospitals and helping with worship. Serving in the seafarers' centres can include bar and shop work, arranging video shows, telephone calls, gardening and cleaning. Recruits approx 24 volunteers annually.

Personal qualities Applicants should be sympathetic and understanding, good at quickly establishing relationships, prepared to befriend people of all nationalities, willing to serve anywhere, and must have an interest in this particular form of ministry.

Age 18-24

Qualifications No specific experience necessary, but the ability to swim and possession of a clean driving licence are required. Applicants must be communicant members of the Church of England, and need references from three suitable people.

Length of service 1 year, starting September.

Terms Board and lodging, travel costs, medical/accident insurance and £14 pocket money per week provided. Three weeks holiday per year.

Briefing Weekend training session arranged.

When to apply As soon as possible.

Publications Two newspapers *Flying Angel News* and *The Sea. Prayer Union* booklet provides details about ports and personnel.

NATIONAL COUNCIL OF YMCAS

Address 640 Forest Road, London E17 3DZ Tel 01-520 5599

Contact The Head of the Education & Programme Development Department

Country USA

Organisation A charity founded in 1844 which works with young people from all walks of life to encourage them to live full and worthwhile lives and develop their potential, to show them that alongside love, care and understanding there exists a hope for the future which is manifested in the life of Jesus Christ. The YMCA is part of a worldwide movement of over 26 million members in 96 countries.

Opportunities A limited number of volunteers are recruited to work as counsellors in children's and young people's outdoor pursuits camps in the USA. The centres are open to all young people regardless of their race, colour or creed and the work includes pastoral care as well as helping organise camp activities. Very occasionally, there are opportunities to help organise workcamps in developing countries.

Personal qualities Working as a camp counsellor is a position of great responsibility and only applicants with a mature approach, patience, understanding and a willingness to give of themselves, are accepted.

Age 21+

Qualifications Competition is very high for places and relevant skills and experience are essential. All nationalities considered. Fluent English required. **HVC**

Length of service 1 year

Terms Accommodation, pocket money, insurance and travel provided.

Briefing Orientation courses arranged where necessary; advice and debriefing can be provided on return.

When to apply Recruitment all year.

Publications Annual Review.

THE PEOPLE-TO-PEOPLE HEALTH
FOUNDATION INC

Address Project Hope, Health Sciences Education Center, Millwood, VA 22646, USA Tel 837 2100

Contact The Recruitment Coordinator

Countries Africa: Egypt, Swaziland. Caribbean: Antigua, Haiti, Jamaica. Europe: Portugal. Far East: People's Republic of China. Latin America: Belize, Costa Rica, El Salvador, Guatemala, Honduras, Panama.

Organisation An independent, non-profit corporation founded in 1958 to provide assistance to developing countries in order to alleviate health care manpower shortages. The principal activity of the Foundation is Project HOPE (Health Opportunity for People Everywhere) where health personnel in developing nations are taught modern techniques of medicine, nursing, dentistry and allied health care.

Opportunities There are vacancies for short-term teaching fellows in medical and nursing schools. Educators work with their host counterparts to upgrade teaching skills in various health care professions. Eventually HOPE-trained personnel assume full responsibility for teaching and treating in self-supporting health care programmes.

Personal qualities Applicants should have a committed interest in international health care training programmes.

Qualifications Professional and academic credentials, such as a degree in a medical field, doctorate or masters degrees, as well as teaching experience frequently required. All nationalities considered. Knowledge of languages needed depending on host country.

Length of service 2 months minimum.

Terms Housing, insurance and travel provided. Pocket money provision varies depending on host country. 40 hour week.

Briefing Debriefing service provided on return.

When to apply Recruitment all year.

Publications *Health Affairs*; *Hope News*.

THE PROJECT TRUST

Address Breacachadh Castle, Isle of Coll, Argyll PA78 6TB
Tel Coll 444

Contact The Administrator

Countries Africa: Egypt, Kenya, South Africa, Sudan, Transkei, Zimbabwe. Asia: India, Sri Lanka. Far East: Hong Kong, Indonesia. Australia; Honduras; Jamaica; Jordan.

Organisation Founded in 1968, a non-sectarian educational trust sending British school leavers overseas for a year between school and further education or commerce/industry. Its aims are to enable a new generation to experience life and work overseas, gaining some understanding of life outside Europe, particularly in the Third World and to place volunteers in a way which is of real benefit to the community.

Opportunities Projects are specifically chosen to ensure that the volunteer is not taking work from an unemployed local person. Opportunities include teaching English, arts and sciences, acting as teacher aides or helping at Outward Bound schools; looking after children in homes for the deprived or handicapped; in hospitals, undertaking medical work and health lectures or caring for leprosy patients; and as jackaroos at sheep or cattle stations. Recruits 130 volunteers annually.

Personal qualities Applicants should have initiative, commonsense, flexibility and sensitivity. They should be physically fit and healthy to cope with the climate and conditions.

Age Minimum 17.3 years, maximum 19 at time of going overseas.

Qualifications No academic qualifications required, except on rare occasions; applicants must be in full-time education and UK citizens holding a British passport.

Length of service One year, starting August/September.

Terms Volunteers live in the same type of accommodation as a local worker, with food usually provided. Insurance, travel and £25 per month pocket money paid. Leave is at the discretion of the host country. Cost £1700, of which the volunteer must raise £1150 through sponsors and earn £100 by themselves. Advice given on obtaining sponsorship.

Briefing Initial interviews held October-January at a location close to the applicant's home; between December and April successful candidates attend a four day selection course on the Isle of Coll, costing £75 plus travel and deductable from sponsorship money. The island's few inhabitants play a major role in the selection and training of volunteers and this plus the history of Coll give volunteers an invaluable insight into the conditions to be met overseas. Compulsory 2 week training course in July; candidates learn the rudiments of teaching and are briefed on their project. Two day debriefing course on return and encouragement to join the Returned Volunteers Association.

When to apply Early application advised; apply by 1 January latest.

Publications *Project Post* quarterly; Annual Report; information leaflets.

QUAKER PEACE AND SERVICE

Address Friends House, Euston Road, London NW1 2BJ Tel 01-387 3601

Contact The Europe Section

Countries Austria, France, Federal Republic of Germany

Organisation The Religious Society of Friends Service Department is committed to working for peace, justice and reconciliation, against violence and poverty and on behalf of the disadvantaged. Volunteers are recruited on behalf of four charities: Evangelisches Diakoniewerk (Austria), Annee Diaconale (France) and Stiftung Sozialer Friedensdienst Pfalz and Diakonie Jahr (Germany).

Opportunities A limited number of volunteers are needed to help in church-run centres and homes with mentally and physically handicapped children and adults, the socially disturbed and the elderly, providing general care and companionship.

Personal qualities Applicants should have a readiness both to give and gain from the placement, evidence of commitment to voluntary service for the disadvantaged and an interest in spending a year abroad. If not Quakers, volunteers are expected to be in sympathy with Friends' views.

Age 18+

Qualifications O/A level or equivalent French or German required. Former experience with children, the elderly or handicapped in an institutional setting an advantage. All nationalities considered. **HVC**

Length of service 1 year, September-August.

Terms Self-catering, semi-independent accommodation, medical insurance and AS1200, FF500 or DM200 per month pocket money provided. 40 hour week. Travel paid by participants. Advice given on obtaining sponsorship.

Briefing One week compulsory orientation course arranged at the Quaker College, Birmingham. In addition, volunteers are visited at least once by QP&S staff during the year, and attend seminars organised by the host organisations. Returned volunteers attend a weekend reunion and debriefing.

When to apply As soon as possible.

Publications *Quaker Peace and Service Reporter* magazine.

REGGIO TERZO MUNDO

Address Via San Girolamo 24, 42100 Reggio Emilia, Italy Tel 38675

Contact The Secretary

Countries Africa: Central African Republic, Madagascar.

Organisation Founded in 1973, it prepares and sends volunteers to the Third World with the aim of fostering technical advancement. Since its foundation, has recruited over 5000 volunteers.

Opportunities Volunteers are needed in the fields of medicine, nursing, physiotherapy, building and agriculture. Recruits 100 volunteers annually.

Personal qualities Applicants should be inspired by Roman Catholic motivation, a spirit of sacrifice, and the ability to develop one's technical skills.

Age 18+

Qualifications Relevant qualifications and experience necessary. All nationalities considered. Knowledge of Italian or French required.

Length of service 2 years

Terms Volunteers live on site with other missionaries.
Insurance and travel provided. 45 hour week.

Briefing Orientation course arranged at headquarters.
Advice on resettlement provided for returned volunteers.

When to apply Recruitment all year.

Publications *Reggio Missioni*

THE RICHMOND FELLOWSHIP

Address 8 Addison Road, London W14 8DL Tel 01-603 6373

Contact The Personnel Officer

Countries Hong Kong; India; Israel; USA.

Organisation A charity founded in 1959 with the principal aim of promoting better understanding of human relations, in particular those factors which tend to foster mental health or lead to emotional disturbance. Carries out a programme of education based on and linked with a therapeutic programme, bringing together people who have suffered emotional distress and people of the area who are concerned in bringing about integration and mutually rewarding relationships. The Fellowships run halfway houses for children, adolescents, young people, families, older people, those diagnosed as schizophrenic, recovering alcoholics, ex-drug users and people needing minimal support. Also provides training courses and a consultative service. Member of the Richmond Fellowship International with branches in 8 countries.

Opportunities Volunteers are needed to work with the emotionally disturbed and, in addition to helping with the practical necessities of life, are involved in activities which include gardening, cooking, art, music, woodwork, decoration and drama groups, sport and relaxation. There are also opportunities for administrative workers. On the American eastern seaboard there are four houses for adolescents, one for senior citizens, one for young adults and a model unit which also serves as a training centre. The establishments in Hong Kong, India and Israel all serve as halfway houses for ex-mental patients.

Personal qualities Applicants should have the commitment to do a very difficult and demanding but rewarding job, and the ability to relate sensitively and sensibly to the residents.

Age 24+

Qualifications Applicants should have some experience with the emotionally disturbed and field or residential social work, depending on the work. Skills in recreational activities an advantage. All nationalities considered.

Length of service 1 year

Terms Volunteers are expected to accept the obligations and responsibilities which apply to staff members, including professional relationship with residents, responsibility within the structure, punctuality and codes of practice. Board and lodging, allowance and sometimes travel provided. 6 day, 48 hour week. 26 days annual leave.

Briefing Induction programme. The leaving process is carefully planned as much for the sake of residents as for the volunteer.

When to apply Recruitment all year.

Publications Annual Report; *Mental Health and the Community: Report of the Richmond Fellowship Enquiry, 1983.*

THE SALVATION ARMY SERVICE CORPS

Address National Headquarters, 101 Queen Victoria Street, London
EC4P 4EP Tel 01-236 5222
In Scotland: Territorial Headquarters, Houldsworth Street, Glasgow
G3 8DU Tel 041-221 3378

Contact London: The Service Corps Officer. Glasgow: The Territorial
Youth Secretary.

Countries Third World countries in Africa, Asia, Caribbean, Far East,
Latin America, Pacific; also limited opportunities in Europe.

Organisation Founded in 1974, a group of people, Christian friends and
Salvationists of all ages, prepared to give service.
It exists to explore opportunities for paid or voluntary full-time lay service
with the Salvation Army and to recruit and place personnel for specific
vacancies in cooperation with international and associated headquarters.

Opportunities A limited number of volunteers are required to work
within the educational, medical, social, evangelical and administrative
branches. There are opportunities for teachers in primary, intermediate
and secondary schools, teacher training colleges, agricultural and
industrial training schools, and schools for the blind and physically
handicapped. Medical staff required include doctors, nurses,
pharmacists, laboratory technicians, radiographers, physiotherapists and
administrative personnel in hospitals, dispensaries and clinics.
Agriculture and village community projects need carpenters, engineers
and mechanics. There are sometimes vacancies for computing,
accountancy and secretarial staff.

Personal qualities Identifying closely with the aims and programmes of
the Salvation Army, applicants should have a concern for the spiritual and
social welfare of people and a capacity for hard work in the cause of
Christ. They should be prompted by a spirit of service and self-sacrifice,
offering to serve the Lord in the capacity for which they are best suited
and in any place where there are needs to be met.

Age 21+

Qualifications Academic and professional qualifications needed vary
according to the position and the location.
Experience required in most cases. Applicants must be British.

Length of service 3 years, renewable by mutual agreement.

Terms Board and lodging in SA centres or living quarters with self-
catering. Salary equivalent to that of a SA officer in the accepting country.
Return travel paid, including dependents if appropriate. One month leave
per year of completed service on return. Observance of teetotalism, non-
smoking, and non-use of addictive drugs required.

Briefing Information provided for orientation. Courses sometimes
arranged. Debriefing and resettlement grant on return.

When to apply Recruitment all year.

Publications Service Corps leaflets.

SIM INTERNATIONAL

Address Joint Mission Centre, Ullswater Crescent, Coulsdon, Surrey CR3 2HR Tel 01-660 7778

Contact The Candidate Secretary

Countries Africa: Benin, Burkina Faso, Ethiopia, Ghana, Ivory Coast, Kenya, Liberia, Niger, Nigeria, Sudan.
Latin America: Bolivia, Peru.

Organisation An international organisation founded in 1893 as the Sudan Interior Mission, it is composed of evangelicals drawn from many different denominations. It serves the Church of Jesus Christ in facilitating the fulfillment of His command to preach the Gospel and to glorify God through church planting. In conjunction with mission-related church bodies and other organisations, its ministries include evangelical outreach, theological education, famine and disaster relief, rural and community development, health care, and youth and literacy programmes.

Opportunities Personnel are generally required in development work for agriculturalists, engineers, water specialists and construction engineers; trades such as electricians and plumbers; medical and medical auxiliary duties; broadcasting and office work; youth work in urban areas; and teaching at schools for missionaries' children.

Personal qualities Applicants must have a commitment to the Lord Jesus Christ and ministry skills. They should be able to work on initiative and have the strength to surmount loneliness, cultural differences, financial limitations and other frustrations. Working as members of a team, they should have the ability to live, work and worship in close proximity to their co-missionaries. Stamina and good health essential.

Age Mid 20s

Qualifications Most host countries require specific skills and experience. Bible training necessary; Christian education and youth work experience desirable. Missionaries usually learn the language of the people among whom they work and, as necessary, the official language of the country. All nationalities considered.

Length of service Open-ended commitment. Short-term service 12-30 months; special service up to 1 year. Summer missionaries usually stay for 2/3 months, but the period may be extended by mutual agreement.

Terms Self-catering house/flat accommodation and insurance provided. All funds including travel to the host country must be raised by the participant. Advice given on obtaining sponsorship.

Briefing Compulsory Candidate Orientation School held twice yearly in London, lasting approx one week, when the volunteer's readiness for service is evaluated in depth. Debriefing interviews on return.

When to apply Applications should be made before the end of the preceding calendar year, preferably in October.

Publications *SIM Now* bi-monthly magazine.

SOUTH AMERICAN MISSIONARY SOCIETY

Address Allen Gardiner House, Pembury Road, Tunbridge Wells, Kent TN2 3QU Tel Tunbridge Wells 38647

Contact The Personnel Secretary

Countries Latin America: Chile, Paraguay, Peru.

Organisation Founded in 1844, the Society exists to encourage and enable the spreading of the Gospel of the Lord Jesus Christ in Latin America and the Iberian Peninsula through partnership with Anglican and other churches, and to initiate and respond to opportunities by mutual sharing of prayer, personnel and resources, with the purpose of being a servant, partner and communication bridge in response to Christ's commission to live out the Gospel among all people.

Opportunities A very limited number of volunteers are required to teach at St Andrew's College, Asuncion, Paraguay; St Paul's School, Vina del Mar, Chile; and the British School, Punta Arenas, Chile; plus working as a Bishop's assistant in Peruvian shanty towns.

Personal qualities Volunteers must have a Christian commitment.

Age 20+

Qualifications Basic 4 week TEFL course important for all accepted candidates. They should have three years teaching experience in either infant or junior schools and a knowledge of Spanish. Applicants must be British citizens.

Length of service 6 months to 1 year.

Terms Accommodation provided with other missionaries or with a host family. No pocket money, insurance or travel provided, but some help given towards obtaining sponsorship.

Briefing Orientation not compulsory, but is sometimes arranged for long-term missionaries. Possible advice/debriefing provided by giving a contact name on return.

When to apply Recruitment all year.

Publications *Share* quarterly newsletter; information leaflets.

TEAR FUND

Address 100 Church Road, Teddington, Middlesex TW11 8QE
Tel 01-977 9144

Contact The Director of Overseas Personnel

Countries Africa: Chad, Ethiopia, Guinea-Bissau, Kenya, Malawi, Mali, Niger, Nigeria, Rwanda, Somalia, Sudan, Tanzania, Uganda, Zaire.
Asia: Bangladesh, Central Asia, India, Nepal, Pakistan.
Caribbean: Haiti. Far East: Indonesia, Thailand.
Latin America: Chile, Paraguay, Peru. Middle East: Lebanon.
Pacific: Philippines.

Organisation Launched in 1968 as The Evangelical Alliance Relief Fund, TEAR Fund became an independent charitable organisation in 1971, providing assistance for the development and emergency relief work of national churches, other Christian agencies and missionary societies in their work among the poor and needy. Its operations have been extended to include development grants, the sending of personnel overseas, individual sponsorship of children and students, handicraft marketing and support for evangelism and Christian education.

Opportunities The main fields of work in which volunteers share their expertise are health care, technical training and agriculture. Nurses, doctors, midwives, nutritionists, occupational therapists, administrators and other medical professionals are needed to work in hospitals, clinics, refugee camps and villages to assist in the provision of community health care programmes, training health assistants and the supply and distribution of medical goods. Technical and trade instructors are required to teach and supervise carpentry, masonry, construction, machine maintenance, engineering, tailoring, managerial and administrative skills, and small business creation, especially in handicrafts. Agricultural specialists are needed to introduce new techniques, run seed schemes and initiate irrigation and water improvement projects. Also opportunities for pastoral and evangelical work.

Personal qualities Applicants should have a Christian commitment to their work.

Age 20+

Qualifications Relevant qualifications, work experience and an aptitude to learn languages essential. All nationalities considered. **HVC**

Length of service 2-4 years

Terms Accommodation arrangements vary depending on the country. Travel, insurance and personal allowance provided.

Briefing Compulsory orientation course arranged. Volunteers write a report for headquarters and are interviewed on their return.

When to apply Recruitment all year.

Publications *Tear Times* quarterly magazine; *Christian at Work Overseas* training manual; *Prayer Diary* quarterly; information leaflets.

UNITED KINGDOM FOUNDATION FOR THE PEOPLES OF THE SOUTH PACIFIC

Address Edward King House, The Old Palace, Lincoln LN2 1PU
Tel Lincoln 28778

Contact The Secretary

Countries Pacific: Fiji, Micronesia, Papua New Guinea, Solomon Islands, Tonga, Vanuatu.

Organisation The European branch of a worldwide organisation dedicated to supporting projects and programmes in the island nations of the South Pacific in their struggle against poverty, malnutrition, disease, leprosy and lack of education.

Opportunities Volunteers are needed to provide labour and technical help, give management and accounting support and secretarial help in village development projects; health, nutrition and sanitation programmes; education, training and community development projects; agriculture, fisheries and animal husbandry; small business, craft centre and cooperative creation; and building projects involving carpentry, joinery, mechanics and boat building. Most of the projects are managed by the respective national development trusts.

Personal qualities Applicants should display a concern for development and a sensitivity to the needs for self-reliance in a volunteer situation.

Age 20+

Qualifications Relevant qualifications are essential; suitable background required for managerial support. All nationalities considered. A good command of English necessary; French is needed for Vanuatu.

Length of service Normally 6-12 months.

Terms Volunteers receive basic accommodation and an allowance. Insurance arrangements are negotiated according to service plan. Participants are encouraged to obtain sponsorship for travel costs, although these may be met from project budgets.

Briefing Compulsory orientation course arranged. The Canadian and US offices have a sophisticated record of debriefing and helping returned volunteers, from which UK volunteers also benefit.

When to apply Recruitment all year.

Publications Annual Report; conference reports; information leaflets.

UNITED NATIONS ASSOCIATION INTERNATIONAL SERVICE

Address 3 Whitehall Court, London SW1A 2EL Tel 01-930 0679

Contact The Administrative Officer

Countries Africa: Burkina Faso, Cape Verde Islands, Mali.
Middle East: West Bank. Latin America: Bolivia, Brazil, Paraguay.

Organisation A voluntary body founded in 1957 which aims to increase awareness of international issues in Britain, campaigning for disarmament, a fairer world economic order and respect by governments for the human rights of their citizens. It sends skilled personnel to work in certain Third World countries for community-based organisations which are working on projects for a fundamental change in the distribution of wealth and power.
BVP

Opportunities There have been recent vacancies for nurses, midwives, occupational therapists, nursery development workers, community workers and nutritionists. Also work for agriculturalists, agronomists, technicians, engineers, literacy workers, project evaluators, librarians, teachers and technical instructors, computer operators, development economists and social researchers. Each posting is defined with care and candidates are matched against the project's needs.

Personal qualities Applicants must have an understanding of development issues, in order to strengthen local development groups and help increase understanding between peoples.
Participants need to have initiative and adaptability to new ways of working and living.

Age 18+. No upper age limit; applications from retired people in good health welcome.

Qualifications Relevant qualifications, working experience and skills required. Third World and community work experience an advantage. Knowledge of the relevant foreign language or the ability to learn a language essential. Couples without dependent children welcome providing both partners have skills or qualifications acceptable to the programme and can be posted together. Applicants must be British or resident in Britain. **HVC**

Length of service 2 years minimum; usual length of service 3 years.

Terms Accommodation, usually in shared self-contained flats, clothing allowance and maintenance allowance or payment related to local salaries provided. Superannuation and National Insurance commitments are paid where applicable and all overseas travel costs are met. 40 hour week. Re-equipment grant made to returned volunteers.

Briefing Compulsory one month orientation course. Language training given as appropriate. One week advice/debriefing service on return.

When to apply Applications should be made well in advance, as acceptance is subject to final approval by the host country.

Publications Annual Review; information leaflets.

UNITED NATIONS VOLUNTEERS

Address Palais des Nations, 1211 Geneva 10, Switzerland Tel 98 58 50

In UK apply to: Voluntary Service Overseas, VSO with UNV Scheme, 9 Belgrave Square, London SW1X 8PW Tel 01-235 5191

Contact Coordinateur Executif

Countries Over 40 countries in Africa.
Asia: Afghanistan, Bangladesh, Bhutan, Maldives, Nepal, Pakistan, Sri Lanka.
Caribbean: Antigua, Dominica, Dominican Republic, Grenada, Haiti, Jamaica, Montserrat, Nevis, St Kitts, St Lucia, St Vincent, Trinidad, Tobago.
Far East: People's Republic of China, Indonesia, Laos, Malaysia, Singapore, Thailand.
Latin America: Colombia, Guatemala, Guyana, Honduras, Nicaragua, Panama, Paraguay, Peru.
Middle East: Bahrain, Lebanon, Oman, Syria, Turkey, Yemen Arab Republic.
Pacific: Cook Islands, Fiji, Papua New Guinea, Philippines, Solomon Islands, Tonga, Tuvalu, Vanuatu, Western Samoa.

Organisation Founded in 1970 by the UN General Assembly, its main purposes and objectives are to contribute to development efforts by providing an additional source of qualified and trained manpower; to offer to the UN system and member states the energetic and catalytic contribution of young professionals who are willing to work under volunteer conditions of modest remuneration; to cooperate with Domestic Development Service organisations at both national and regional levels; to provide increased opportunities for young professionals from all nations to contribute to and gain experience in UN-related and national development programmes; and thus to increase international understanding and cooperation. Some 1000 volunteers are serving in nearly 100 developing countries; 80% of volunteers come from developing nations.

Opportunities The programme provides middle and upper-level expertise in areas of administration, communications and transport, engineering, human settlements, education, social/natural sciences, health, skilled trades and other professional fields. Volunteers range from accountants to youth workers, economists to entomologists, geologists to graphic designers, lab technicians to librarians, mechanics to midwives, social workers to statisticians, and other specialists in some 100 professional categories. As development workers UN volunteers offer valuable assistance in fields where skilled manpower is often lacking, and make their skills available to developing countries, helping to train national personnel to carry on the volunteer's work when the assignments have ended.

Personal qualities Candidates must posses the motivation to help others and pass on their skills at a working level.
Volunteers should be able to rely on their own ingenuity in order to work against and surmount the job's inherent difficulties and frustrations. Good health and a willingness and ability to withstand climates and conditions to which the volunteer may not be accustomed are desirable.

continued overleaf

Age 21+, but most volunteers are at least 25.

Qualifications A degree or technical diploma required, plus a minimum of 2 years relevant work experience; for volunteers in certain skilled trades, professional experience substitutes for advanced degrees. Married candidates with or without children are welcome, but are often difficult to place. Most nationalities considered. Languages needed include French, Spanish, Arabic and Portuguese. **HVC**

Length of service 2 years minimum

Terms Provisions are made to ensure availability of modest accommodation and a settling-in grant helps volunteers to establish themselves in a new home with purchases of household items. Monthly allowance provided to cover modest living expenses at either single or dependancy rates, which varies in each country of assignment. Volunteers and their dependents receive health insurance and travel costs.

Briefing Briefing in Geneva or at the HQ of the UN executing agency involved and at the UN Development Programme office in the country of assignment.

When to apply Recruitment all year.

Publications *UNV Newsletter* quarterly; *World Statistical Directory of Volunteer and Development Service Organisations* biennial. Other publications include: *UNV List of Vacant Posts*; *UNV Sample List of Candidates*; and special reports.

THE UNITED REFORMED CHURCH

Address 86 Tavistock Place, London WC1H 9RT Tel 01-837 7661

Contact The Secretary for Personnel

Countries Africa: Botswana, Madagascar, Zambia, Zimbabwe.
Asia: Bangladesh, India. Caribbean: Jamaica.
Far East: Hong Kong, Taiwan. Pacific: Kiribati, Papua New
Guinea, Solomon Islands, Western Samoa.

Organisation Founded in 1972, a member of the Council for World
Mission. Meets staffing requests from overseas partner churches for their
projects. It is also involved in the international exchange of ministers.

Opportunities Most requests are for lay missionaries working as
secondary teachers, theological educators, doctors, nurses, mechanics,
accountants and occasionally administrators. They work alongside local
people and are generally expected to run training programmes which
allow national staff to assume greater responsibility and, eventually, run
the schools, health centres and offices themselves.

Personal qualities Applicants should have a willingness to learn from
overseas workers, a sincerity in believing that they can receive as well as
share their skills and a desire to share in the life and work of the partner
churches.

Age 22+

Qualifications Relevant qualifications, a few years of professional
experience and a knowledge of relevant languages required. All
nationalities considered.

Length of service 2 years minimum.

Terms Accommodation and salary in line with local workers, return travel
and insurance provided by the overseas church.

Briefing Compulsory preparation and orientation course lasts a maximum
of one year. Personal advice and help with reintegration is given on
return and, occasionally, specialist in-service and debriefing courses can
be arranged.

When to apply Recruitment all year.

Publications Information leaflet.

THE UNITED SOCIETY FOR THE PROPAGATION OF THE GOSPEL

Address USPG House, 15 Tufton Street, London SW1P 3QQ Tel 01-222 4222

Contact Personnel Department, Mission Programmes Division

Countries Experience Exchange Programme: Africa: Lesotho, South Africa, Swaziland, Tanzania. Asia: India, Pakistan. Far East: Malaysia. Latin America: Argentina, Brazil, Uruguay.
Skills-in-Action: Africa: Malawi, Tanzania, Zambia, Zimbabwe. Asia: India, Pakistan, Sri Lanka. Caribbean.

Organisation Founded in 1701, the Society enables the Church of England to relate effectively to Anglican Churches throughout the world and to support the work of overseas churches by offering them personnel, funding and bursaries.

Opportunities The Experience Exchange Programme was established to enable Christians from the UK to learn from the insights and experiences of Christians in other countries. Volunteer placements, agreed by local Anglican bishops and leaders of Christian community projects, assist in schools, medical centres, social welfare and agricultural projects. Recruits 20 volunteers annually.
In Skills-In-Action local Anglican church leaders and heads of institutions make requests for skilled volunteers in the medical, paramedical, nursing, teaching, agricultural, technical, pastoral, administration, accountancy, crafts, construction and mechanical areas of work. Recruits 25 volunteers annually.

Personal qualities Participants must be mature practising Christians with an interest and commitment in identifying with a local Christian community. They should also be adaptable to new situations, resourceful, sensitive to people and willing to suffer some hardship and loneliness.

Age EEP: 18+. SIA: 20+

Qualifications British applicants only. EEP: No special qualifications or experience necessary. SIA: Appropriate qualifications and some relevant experience essential.

Length of service EEP: 6-12 months usually commencing in the autumn. SIA: 18-24 months.

Terms EEP: Volunteers pay their fares and insurance, and contribute to board and lodging costs. Advice given on obtaining sponsorship. SIA: Board, accommodation, local allowance and assistance towards travel costs provided. Financial contributions are assessed on personal circumstances; participants are encouraged to obtain sponsorship.

Briefing Compulsory orientation courses arranged, with advice and debriefing on return.

When to apply Recruitment all year.

Publications *Network* quarterly magazine; *Mission Calling* regular vacancies list; information leaflets.

UNIVERSITIES' EDUCATIONAL FUND FOR PALESTINIAN REFUGEES

Address 63 Holbrook Road, Cambridge CB1 4SX Tel Cambridge 248473

Contact The Volunteer Programme Coordinator

Countries Israeli-occupied West Bank and Gaza Strip; Palestinian communities in Israel and the Lebanon; occasionally Jordan and elsewhere in the Middle East.

Organisation Founded in 1972 UNIPAL is a small educational charity which aims to provide forms of help which will benefit not only individuals but also Palestinian communities and especially over 700,000 refugees still in camps. Palestinian nurses and teachers of English are brought to the UK for training; financial aid is given to Palestinian educational institutions that are helping deprived children and young people; and volunteers are sent to the Middle East to share their skills.

Opportunities A strictly limited number of volunteers are needed. Work for medium-term volunteers generally involves helping in children's homes and kindergartens; long-term volunteers teach science or English as a foreign language and, occasionally, there are openings for secretaries, physio/occupational therapists, midwives and nurses. For short-term opportunities see *Working Holidays*.

Personal qualities Sensitivity, tolerance, readiness to learn, political awareness, adaptability and a sense of responsibility are needed.

Age 20-40

Qualifications Qualifications and previous relevant experience necessary. Background reading on the Middle East situation essential.

Length of service 3 months minimum, longer preferred. 1 academic year minimum for teachers.

Terms Food and simple shared accommodation provided. Volunteers serving over 6 months receive fares, insurance and pocket money. Registration fee £5.

Briefing Interviews are held and successful applicants are then briefed on their placement.

When to apply Apply by January.

Publications Information leaflets.

VIATORES CHRISTI

Address 9 Harcourt Terrace, Dublin 2, Ireland Tel Dublin 76 30 50

Contact The Secretary

Countries Anywhere in the world but mostly in developing countries.
Africa: Ethiopia, Gambia, Ghana, Kenya, Liberia, Malawi, Nigeria, Sierra Leone, South Africa, Tanzania, Zambia, Zimbabwe.
Asia: India, Pakistan. Caribbean: Grenada, Haiti.
Far East: Thailand. Latin America: Chile, Venezuela.
There are usually some volunteers involved in areas of need in Europe and North America, eg among the Indian population of British Columbia, Canada.

Organisation Founded in 1960, a lay missionary organisation in outlook dedicated to the active involvement of Catholic laity in the missionary work of the Church, with the task of recruiting, training and helping to place laity overseas in areas of need. It has the object of furthering the Church's work, of bringing Christ to all men everywhere, and in sharing skills in the process.

Opportunities The most frequent requests are for teachers of all subjects; medical personnel including doctors, nurses, and laboratory technicians; social workers; catechists; agriculturalists; and mechanics, carpenters, builders, electricians and engineers. Some volunteers work as full-time pastoral, development or youth workers playing an active part in the local Christian community. Volunteers fulfill a specific task, usually in which they have training or experience, passing on their skills so that local people will be able to continue when they leave.

Personal qualities Volunteers should be concerned, caring and practising Catholics with a desire to share in Christ's mission and spread the Gospel. They should be open to learn, before going and whilst overseas, adaptable, have a sense of humour, be in good health and generally suited to the work to be done. Whether single or married, applicants should be free of family or other commitments.

Age 21 +, but training can be given before this.

Qualifications Relevant skills and previous experience preferred. Applicants must be resident in Ireland to attend training course.

Length of service 1-2 years.

Terms Conditions depend on the requesting agency. Insurance, travel and, usually, board and lodging provided. Advice given on sponsorship.

Briefing Much emphasis is placed on the preparation programme, and comprises Christian formation, orientation and practical experience. Compulsory part-time orientation course arranged lasting 6-12 months, depending on the individual's readiness and availability of a suitable post. As a debriefing service, residential weekends and seminars are held where experiences are shared; home involvement is invited.

When to apply Recruitment all year.

Publications International newsletter; Annual Report.

VOLUNTARY SERVICE OVERSEAS

Address 9 Belgrave Square, London SW1X 8PW Tel 01-235 5191

Contact The Director

Countries Africa: Burundi, Egypt, Gambia, Ghana, Kenya, Liberia, Malawi, Nigeria, Rwanda, Sierra Leone, Sudan, Tanzania, Uganda, Zambia, Zimbabwe.
Asia: Bangladesh, Bhutan, Maldives, Nepal, Sri Lanka.
Caribbean: Anguilla, Antigua, Dominica, Grenada, Montserrat, St Kitts, St Lucia, St Vincent, Turks and Caicos.
Far East: People's Republic of China, Indonesia, Malaysia, Thailand. Latin America: Belize.
Pacific: Fiji, Kiribati, Papua New Guinea, Philippines, Solomon Islands, Tonga, Tuvalu, Vanuatu.

Organisation An independent organisation founded in 1958 with the aim of transferring practical experience, skills and expertise to the developing countries in their fight against poverty, disease and malnutrition. A movement of people who share a basic belief that practical action by individuals can contribute significantly to this objective and so assist independent development and the attainment of social and economic justice. Volunteers with relevant skills or qualifications are sent at the specific request of governments and local employers overseas, so that local counterparts can carry on the work once the volunteer's term of service expires. Volunteers are only sent to schemes which demonstrably help the appropriate community concerned, and all requests are evaluated against firmly established project criteria. There are more than 500 volunteers overseas at any one time working on projects in 40 Third World countries. **BVP**

Opportunities The majority of requests are in the following fields. Primary, secondary and tertiary education: TEFL, teacher training, librarianship, special education, home economics, commerce and science. Health: midwives, doctors, physiotherapists, health visitors, community nurses, pharmacists, dentists, laboratory technicians, occupational/speech therapists and nutritionists. Technical trades, crafts and engineering: carpenters, bricklayers, joiners, plumbers, electricians, building instructors, mechanics, marine/civil engineers, technicians and technical teachers. Agriculture: livestock and crop specialists, foresters, agricultural engineers, horticulturalists, animal health and production specialists, fisheries experts and agricultural science teachers. Social, community and business development: advisors to help set up small businesses, establish craft workshops and cottage industries, community social workers and instructors working with the disabled, town planners and architects, communications experts, computer programmers, journalists and solicitors.

Personal qualities Applicants should have a genuine desire to assist in the long-term development of the Third World. They should be adaptable, prepared for life in a completely different culture, resilient in the face of frustrations, tolerant, have a sense of humour and a desire to combat all forms of exploitation.

Age 20-65; most are in their late 20s

continued overleaf

Qualifications Relevant qualifications and experience essential. Couples without dependent children welcome, provided both partners have skills or qualifications acceptable to the programme and can be posted together. Volunteers should be living in the UK with unrestricted right of re-entry. **HVC**

Length of service 2 years minimum.

Terms Accommodation provided by the host country. Volunteers live and work as members of the community, alongside their colleagues on similar pay. Air fare and other travel expenses, National Insurance contributions and payments to a specially arranged endowment plan plus medical insurance are provided. A further grant is paid on return.

Briefing Compulsory 10 day course in which volunteers learn to adapt their skills to the needs of the host country, with briefing on the country, health care and any special training they may need by nationals and returned volunteers. Debriefing and advice on resettlement provided on return.

When to apply Recruitment all year; most volunteers are sent out in September and January.

Publications *Orbit* quarterly magazine; Annual Review; information literature.

THE VOLUNTEER MISSIONARY MOVEMENT

Address Shenley Lane, London Colney, St Albans, Hertfordshire
AL2 1AR Tel Bowmansgreen 24853

Contact The Regional Director

Countries Africa: Bophutatswana, Ethiopia, Ghana, Kenya, Liberia,
Malawi, Nigeria, Sierra Leone, Sudan, Tanzania, Uganda, Zambia,
Zimbabwe. Pacific: Papua New Guinea.

Organisation Founded in 1969 following the Second Vatican Council, an
ecumenical movement within the Catholic Church which recruits,
prepares and sends Christian volunteers with a skill or profession to work
as lay missionaries in Catholic or other Christian mission projects linked
with local churches. It is also involved in long-term development projects,
mission awareness and development education in the UK.

Opportunities Skilled volunteers are required to work on educational,
agricultural, preventive health care, community development, home
economics and vocational training projects.
There are opportunities for teachers, particularly of maths, science,
English and commercial subjects; agriculturalists; doctors and
nurses/midwives; carpenters, builders, plumbers and electricians;
accountants and administrators. Most volunteers work in rural areas which
may be isolated, with limited social amenities. Recruits 50 volunteers
annually.

Personal qualities Applicants must be practising Christians with a
concern for people and a desire to serve overseas motivated by Christian
faith. They need to be adaptable, stable and patient, capable of working
independently, good at improvisation and with a sense of humour.

Age 21+; no upper age limit.

Qualifications Volunteers must have technical or professional
qualifications with at least one year's post-qualification experience.
Married couples without school age children accepted provided both are
suitably qualified and available for work. All nationalities considered.
HVC

Length of service 2 years minimum.

Terms Basic accommodation, living allowance and return air fare
provided. Volunteers contribute £60 towards insurance.

Briefing Successful applicants attend weekend introductory course.
Compulsory 5 week residential preparatory course arranged; volunteers
contribute £50 towards cost. Open house for returned volunteers;
weekends and retreats organised.

When to apply Recruitment all year.

Publications Newsletter; *VMM Spirit and Lifestyle* booklet setting out the
Movement's role in the Church. Information leaflets.

WORLD COMMUNITY DEVELOPMENT SERVICE

Address Educational Visits Scheme, 27 Montagu Road, Botley, Oxford OX2 9AH Tel Oxford 725607

Contact The General Secretary

Countries India; Sri Lanka.

Organisation A charitable society founded in 1974, the Service is a group of people who share a commitment to justice and equality and whose activities are primarily educational, aimed at creating a better awareness of life and society in developing countries.

Opportunities Volunteers are needed on mainly rural development projects run by local voluntary organisations, living and working in a local group and involving themselves fully in the project. All are working to tackle poverty in their area; this may involve running nursery schools and adult literacy classes, organising women's groups, training young people, agricultural, environmental and health work, attending village meetings and helping project staff to improve their English. Participants are encouraged to visit other organisations to widen their view of south Asian life and the different approaches to development.

Personal qualities Participants must be able to get on with people, be reasonably literate, self-reliant, resilient, energetic, open-minded and patient; conditions can at times be difficult, frustrating and uncomfortable. Volunteers should have an interest in current affairs, a commitment to learning and using their experiences on return, and a willingness to understand and respect local culture and traditions.

Age At least 17.5; most participants are under 30.

Qualifications No academic qualifications, specific skills or experience necessary. Applicants from outside the UK are welcome, but must attend interviews and orientation in the UK.

Length of service 6-12 months, starting February or September; availability of 12 month placements not guaranteed.

Terms Participants contribute to the cost of a placement, approx £810-£850, which includes flight, simple local accommodation and vegetarian food, insurance and a small allowance. Fundraising information sheets provided; assistance required thereafter is provided where practicable.

Briefing Selection weekends held with group discussions and the chance to talk to former participants. Successful candidates attend a compulsory 8 day orientation course. Debriefing/discussion weekend organised for each group on return, and meetings are held every 2-3 months; emphasis is placed on the continued participation in the Scheme and the organisation. Membership fee £8; claimants £4.

When to apply By 1 June for September, and by 1 November for February; but no earlier than 9 months before proposed date of departure.

Publications *Forum* six-monthly magazine; information leaflets.

YOUTH EXCHANGE CENTRE

Address Seymour Mews House, Seymour Mews, London W1H 9PE
Tel 01-486 5101

Contact The Training Officer

Country Federal Republic of Germany

Organisation A governmental agency operating a small number of exchange programmes and supporting other exchanges with training, information services and grant aid to youth exchange groups. Will operate a volunteer exchange programme in cooperation with Community Service Volunteers, for an initial two years (1986 and 1987) and, with the agency consortium Freiwilliges Soziales Jahr, cooperate in placing young volunteers in a period of community service.

Opportunities Placements are in hospitals, old people's homes, projects for the handicapped, kindergartens, children's homes, youth hostels, in general church work and other community projects. Volunteers are in close daily contact with people, recognising the social needs of another culture which require different solutions. Recruits a minimum of 20 volunteers annually.

Personal qualities Applicants should show a commitment to community service and a motivation to adapt to the language and culture of the host country.

Age 18-25

Qualifications Candidates must speak German, at least to O level standard. Previous experience desirable but not essential.
British applicants only. **HVC**

Length of service 6 months, March-August.

Terms Volunteers receive board and lodging, necessary local travel expenses, certain insurance, and DM200 minimum per month pocket money. Subsidy provided for a language course if required. 40 hour week. Cost £80; volunteers pay a contribution to seminars and return travel from London, except in certain circumstances. Advice given on obtaining sponsorship.

Briefing Interviews held in London in January by a representative of the German agencies involved. Briefing meeting held before departure. The agencies provide a 1 week orientation course, evaluation weekend, training and support service, and arrange group meetings and seminars.

When to apply Apply by December 21.

Publications Information leaflet.

SECTION II

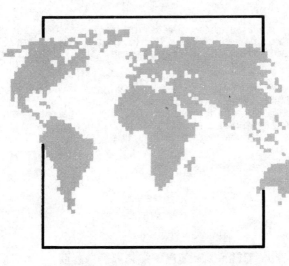

OVERSEAS VOLUNTARY SERVICE
ADVISORY BODIES

CATHOLIC MISSIONARY EDUCATION CENTRE

Address Holcombe House, The Ridgeway, London NW7 4HY Tel 01-906 1642

Organisation Set up by missionary societies in 1972 under the National Missionary Council to act as an information and resource centre to assist the societies in their work of mission education at home with church and church-related organisations.

Advice Disseminates information received from the organisations on volunteer opportunities in the Third World, particularly Africa. Coordinating agency for enquiries from those looking for voluntary work and unsure where to apply.

Publications *Network* annual directory of National Missionary Council members and associates; *Our Resources* a directory of information sources and pastoral help; information graphics: maps, diagrams, work and fact sheets on the churches work in other countries; leaflets, booklets, reports, statistical lists, audio/video cassettes.

CHRISTIANS ABROAD

Address Livingstone House, 11 Carteret Street, London SW1H 9DL Tel 01-222 2165

Organisation An ecumenical body supported by aid and mission agencies providing an information and advisory service on work abroad to help volunteers discover how and through which organisations their skills could be utilised. It exists to encourage lay people to consider whether they have skills that would be welcomed abroad or something to contribute towards development and justice through study and action in the UK.

Advice Any Christians going abroad can be helped with a pre-departure briefing, by sending ahead of them an introduction to a church and by putting them in touch with someone who has worked in the area they are going to. Assistance is offered to those returning from overseas who face the challenge of sharing their experiences and of using what they have learnt, and surmounting the problems of readjustment. A brief description of qualifications, interests and experience should accompany any enquiry.

Publications *A Place for You Overseas* series of leaflets covering opportunities abroad through a variety of organisations and schemes; *Opportunities Abroad* six-monthly list drawing together current vacancies through approx 30 mission and voluntary organisations; *Christians on the Move* booklet giving the experiences of people who have worked abroad; *A Place for You Back in Britain* for returned volunteers.

COORDINATING COMMITTEE FOR INTERNATIONAL VOLUNTARY SERVICE

Address 1 rue Miollis, 75015 Paris, France Tel 568 2732

Organisation A non-governmental international organisation operating within, and founded in 1948 on the initiative of, UNESCO with a membership of over 100 organisations engaged in volunteer work, including those from eastern and western Europe, Latin America, Africa and Asia. Through the promotion and development of the voluntary movement on regional, national and international levels the Committee works towards peace, international understanding, development and the furtherance of the efforts of developing countries in strengthening their national independence, and in solidarity with peoples in observance of the Universal Declaration of Human Rights. It works for the benefit of people affected by all forms of social and economic exploitation, unemployment, bad working and living conditions and promotes awareness and action against these forms of degradation. It organises seminars and conferences, sponsors training courses for volunteer workers, participates in solidarity action and raises funds for concrete projects carried out by voluntary organisations in order to attain genuine development.

Advice It replies to requests for information received from individuals and organisations.

Publications *Directory of Organisations Concerned with International Voluntary Service*; *Volunteering in Literacy Work* a guide to national and international opportunities; *New Trends in Voluntary Service* a review of contemporary developments; *News from CCIVS* regular bulletin; lists of worldwide medium and long-term voluntary service opportunities.

EVANGELICAL MISSIONARY ALLIANCE

Address Whitefield House, 186 Kennington Park Road, London SE11 4BT Tel 01-735 0421

Organisation Founded in 1958, a fellowship of evangelical missionary societies, agencies, training colleges and individuals committed to world mission. Aims to encourage cooperation and provide coordination between member societies and colleges, and assist local churches to fulfill their role in world mission.
Provides a forum in which experiences, ideas and strategy can be shared; groups covering Africa, Asia, China, Europe, Latin America and the Muslim world meet regularly. Missionary exhibitions, conferences, visits and specialist training courses arranged.

Advice As a clearing house for information on world mission it will assist enquirers and direct them to relevant sources.
Also provides information on vacancies among member societies and colleges.

Publications *Missionary Mandate* bi-monthly prayer bulletin; *EMA Bulletin* information digest; pamphlets and books on mission topics.

REGIONAL CONFERENCE ON INTERNATIONAL VOLUNTARY SERVICE

Address Thomas-Mann-Strasse 52, 5300 Bonn 1, Federal Republic of Germany Tel 63 44 24

Organisation Founded in 1964, a coordinating body of over 200 non-governmental organisations which select, train and send out voluntary development workers, or are coordinating or financing such activities. Based in western Europe, it promotes international voluntary service in development cooperation, provides a forum for discussion on a regional level, offers services to its members and encourages joint action in the interest of cooperation in development and international solidarity. Organises colloquia on specific issues of concern to volunteers and volunteer-sending agencies, and, in close association with the Parliamentary Assembly of the Council of Europe, runs regular seminars on important issues in development cooperation. It has been successful in harmonising the conditions of European overseas development workers.

Publications *Newsletter*; *Workers for Development* survey of volunteers from EC non-governmental organisations; reports on colloquia.

RETURNED VOLUNTEER ACTION

Address 1 Amwell Street, London EC1R 1UL Tel 01-278 0804

Organisation The only British organisation of and for prospective, serving and ex-volunteers and others who have worked overseas, existing independently from the sending agencies. It believes that a period of voluntary service abroad fails to achieve its full value unless it becomes part of an educative process for the volunteer, and most of its work involves face to face contacts between more recently returned volunteers and those who have been back for up to two years. Provides information and advice for those thinking about volunteering overseas, a link with volunteers in Europe through Ex-Volunteers International, and helps returned volunteers to make use of their overseas experience in Britain by providing support and advice, training courses in communication skills and a channel through which volunteers can comment on and influence the policies of the sending agencies. **BVP**

Advice Gives advice on all aspects of volunteering abroad and action to take on returning from a period of service.

Publications *Working Overseas* advisory pack containing information on the sending agencies and general advice for the prospective overseas worker, *Questioning Development*, *Handbook for Development Workers Overseas*, *Thinking about Volunteering?* and *The EVI Charter*; *Comeback* quarterly magazine; pamphlets and information sheets.

SECTION III

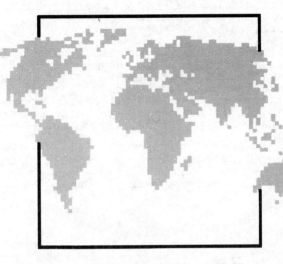

OVERSEAS PROFESSIONAL BODIES

THE BRITISH RED CROSS SOCIETY

Address International Aid Department, 9 Grosvenor Crescent, London SW1X 7EJ Tel 01-235 5454

Organisation Founded in 1870, an independent voluntary organisation and part of a worldwide non-political, non-religious movement based on the fundamental principles of humanitarianism, neutrality and impartiality. As part of the International Red Cross it has a statutory obligation to work for the improvement of health, the prevention of disease and the mitigation of suffering throughout the world.

Opportunities Recruits salaried personnel, mostly qualified and experienced health workers, engineers, nutritionists, mechanics, logistics experts and experienced development workers to work with the International Red Cross usually on emergency relief programmes for the victims of natural disaster and conflict, mainly in Africa and south-east Asia. Salary, accommodation, travel, insurance and field allowance provided; contracts are from 3-18 months. Applicants must be resident in the UK.

Publications *Red Cross News* quarterly newsletter; *The Red Cross Then and Now*; Annual Review; International Red Cross publications concerning relief and development work.

EURO ACTION-ACORD

Address Francis House, Francis Street, London SW1P 1DQ Tel 01-828 7611

Organisation A charity founded in 1976, a consortium of 23 European and Canadian non-governmental organisations whose main role is to respond to development needs in areas of Africa where collective action is deemed more appropriate than separate action by individual member agencies and in circumstances where local agencies are not available for implementation of projects. The consortium is independent of political and religious affiliations, and plans and implements medium and long-term development programmes designed to promote the self-reliance of the communities concerned.

Opportunities Specialists are needed in all aspects of rural development including crop production, animal husbandry, small businesses and cooperatives. Personnel recruited generally have several years experience in the Third World. Reasonable professional salaries with benefits such as free housing, health insurance, annual leave and return travel provided.

Publications Information leaflet.

OVERSEAS DEVELOPMENT ADMINISTRATION

Address Overseas Manpower Services, Abercrombie House, Eaglesham Road, East Kilbride, Glasgow G75 8EA Tel East Kilbride 41199

Organisation Administers the British Government's programme of aid to developing countries, which includes recruitment of skilled staff mostly for the public services of overseas governments. It also assists in the recruitment of specialists for the field programmes of the United Nations and its specialised agencies. **BVP**

Opportunities Recruits professionals in the fields of agriculture, education, accountancy, engineering, cooperative development, law, medicine, customs, economics and science.
Substantial post-qualification experience, preferably overseas, essential in all cases, and applicants must be British.
Salary, allowances, travel, accommodation and paid leave provided; appointments usually last for 2-3 years.

Publications *Why Not Serve Overseas?*, *Opportunities Overseas in International Organisations*, *Opportunities in Education Overseas* booklets; *Overseas Development and Aid* guide to sources of information and material.

OXFAM

Address Personnel Department, 274 Banbury Road, Oxford OX2 7DZ Tel Oxford 56777

Organisation An international agency which exists primarily to provide finance for work to relieve and prevent suffering overseas. It is a partnership of those who believe in the essential dignity of people and their capacity to overcome the problems and pressures which can crush or exploit them, and works for the basic human rights of food, shelter and reasonable conditions of life. It operates by distributing money and resources through other organisations which have their own programmes in the field, and where locally qualified staff are not available, it occasionally recruits qualified specialists.

Opportunities Maintains a Retrieval Register for those looking for 1-4 year contracts with some good village level experience in relief and/or development work plus relevant qualifications, and for specialist personnel prepared to go overseas at short notice either at times of emergency for 3-6 months or sometimes as advisers in, for example, community health/nutrition, agriculture, engineering and social studies projects.

Publications *Oxfam News* quarterly newspaper; *Oxfam Review*; information sheets and leaflets on themes in development, health and country backgrounds; project write-ups; and specialist publications on development issues, agriculture, appropriate technology, health/nutrition and water/sanitation.

SAVE THE CHILDREN FUND

Address Mary Datchelor House, 17 Grove Lane, London SE5 8RD
Tel 01-703 5400

Organisation Founded in 1919, Britain's largest international children's charity is a non-political, independent voluntary organisation, professionally staffed. Basing its work on the Rights of The Child Charter, it is wholly concerned with the rescue in disaster and the longer term welfare of children worldwide in hunger, sickness and need, irrespective of country, nationality, race or religion.

Opportunities Doctors, nurses, health visitors, nutritionists and management staff, including field directors and administrative assistants, are needed in Africa, Asia, Middle East and Latin America. Projects include community health schemes, medical care for refugees, nutrition and feeding programmes, disaster and famine relief, and village development aid. A comprehensive package of salary based on NHS scales, travel and benefits is provided; posts are for 3 months to 2 years.

Publications Annual Report; information literature.

WORLD VISION OF BRITAIN

Address Dychurch House, 8 Abington Street, Northampton NN1 2AJ
Tel Northampton 22964

Organisation Founded in 1950, a branch of World Vision International, an inter-denominational Christian humanitarian organisation dedicated to serving God through child care, emergency relief, community development, evangelism, Christian leadership training and mission challenge. Operates in over 70 countries through local churches and community leaders in close cooperation with the United Nations and other international relief agencies.

Opportunities Recruit professionally qualified, committed Christian doctors, nurses, nutritionists, logisticians, hydro-geologists, civil engineers, water drilling experts and vocational instructors, primarily in Africa and occasionally in South and Central America and Asia. Salary based on US scales, travel and insurance provided; 3 month renewable contracts.

Publications *Window on the World* quarterly magazine; information leaflet.

SECTION IV

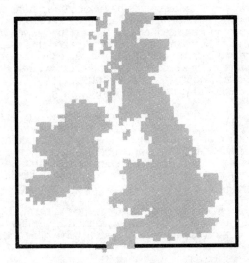

VOLUNTARY SERVICE IN THE UK+IRELAND

RECRUITING AGENCIES

ATD FOURTH WORLD

Address 48 Addington Square, London SE5 7LB Tel 01-703 3231

Contact The General Secretary

Organisation Aide a Toute Detresse is an international movement founded in 1958 in France, and established as a charity in the UK in 1963. Millions of workers and their families have for generations lived in extreme poverty, increasingly dependent on and controlled by others and despite their hopes and efforts they are denied the means of being fully active members of society. In every country these families constitute the Fourth World - ten million people in Europe alone. ATD works alongside the most disadvantaged and excluded families, as well as with all levels in society, to protect and guarantee the fundamental rights of families to family life, education and representation.

Opportunities Workcamps and working weekends are arranged where volunteers work alongside members of the permanent voluntariat, doing building, decorating, gardening, secretarial and translation work at the family centre in Surrey and the national centre in London. For volunteers who are able to stay longer, it is sometimes possible to take part in projects at nurseries, skill centres, libraries, youth and children's clubs and on family holidays as an introduction to the permanent voluntariat.

Personal qualities Applicants should have a genuine interest in learning about the experiences and hopes of very disadvantaged communities as a vital first step to building a future with them, and a willingness to work hard with others as a team.

Age 17+

Qualifications There are no minimum requirements, professionally or academically. Everyone is welcome, including couples with families. All nationalities considered. Knowledge of English required. **HVC**

Length of service An open-ended commitment is preferred if intending to become a member of the permanent voluntariat.

Terms Volunteers on workcamps/working weekends contribute approx £3 per day towards food and accommodation. Permanent voluntariat members are provided with accommodation, food, pocket money after 3 months service and a minimum wage after one year. Accident insurance provided.

Briefing Volunteers receive a full introduction to the work of ATD; evaluation and debriefing sessions are arranged.

When to apply Recruitment all year.

Publications *Fourth World Journal* and *Fourth World Youth Newsletter*; Annual Report; plus numerous Fourth World books.

BIRMINGHAM AND WEST MIDLANDS MARGERY FRY MEMORIAL TRUST

Address 848 Bristol Road, Selly Oak, Birmingham B29 6HW Tel 021-472 0640

Contact The Administration Officer

Organisation Founded in 1959 a housing association and charity which was in the forefront of the establishment of after-care hostels for ex-offenders. As there appears to be a relationship between homelessness and reconviction, the Trust works to provide a safe lodging and an alternative to custody, and thereby a positive framework within which lives may be rebuilt. A positive response to aberrant or destructive behaviour through reconciliation, restitution and reparation is more likely to encourage the good in all parties, restore those who have been damaged, reduce resentment and enable fuller integration.

Opportunities Volunteers are needed to assist in the Trust's six hostels in the Midlands and on committee work. In addition to building up trusting relationships with ex-offenders, there may also be the opportunity to help in the workshop.

Personal qualities Applicants should be in good health, mature and have a sympathetic interest in the care of ex-offenders.

Age 22+

Qualifications Previous experience usually preferred. All nationalities considered. Fluent English essential. **HVC**

Length of service Negotiable; average 3-6 months.

Terms Full board and accommodation usually provided.
Participants are encouraged to obtain sponsorship as they are expected to provide their own pocket money and meet insurance and travel costs.

When to apply Recruitment all year.

Publications Annual Report; information leaflets.

BREAK

Address 20 Hooks Hill Road, Sheringham, Norfolk NR26 8NL
Tel Sheringham 823170

Contact The Director

Organisation A charity founded in 1968, providing holidays, short-stay and emergency care for handicapped and socially deprived children, mentally handicapped adults and families with special needs.

Opportunities Volunteers are needed for residential work at two holiday homes at Sheringham and Hunstanton on the north Norfolk coast. Work as care assistants involves helping with the personal welfare of the guests, their recreational programmes and with essential domestic duties. Placements, involving work discussions and practical assessments, can be arranged for those seeking experience prior to or as part of an educational course leading to qualifications for work with children. Recruits 80-100 volunteers annually.

Personal qualities Applicants should be mature, stable, patient, understanding, conscientious, and able to accept physical and emotional pressures.

Age 17+

Qualifications No qualifications or experience necessary.
All nationalities considered. Good command of English required.

Length of service 3-12 months.

Terms Board, lodging, insurance and £13 per week pocket money provided, plus travel expenses within the UK. 40 hour week.

When to apply Recruitment all year.

THE CAMPHILL VILLAGE TRUST

Address Delrow House, Hilfield Lane, Aldenham, Watford, Hertfordshire WD2 8DJ Tel Radlett 6006

Contact The Secretary

Organisation A charity founded in 1955 which aims to provide a new and constructive way of life for mentally handicapped adults, assisting them to individual independence and social adjustment within the communities of the Trust. It guides them towards open employment while helping them to achieve full integration within society as a whole, by providing a home, work, further education and general care. The centres are based on Rudolf Steiner principles.

Opportunities Volunteers are needed to work alongside the residents in every aspect of communal life at centres where the handicapped can establish themselves, work, and lead a normal family life in a social background. There are three villages offering employment, two town houses for those in open employment, a college, and centres for agriculture, horticulture and assessment. Volunteers work in gardens and farms run on organic principles, craft workshops, bakeries, laundries, printing presses, and participate in the general life and chores of the community. Special emphasis is placed on social, cultural and recreational life.

Personal qualities Applicants should have an interest and understanding in work with the mentally handicapped and be prepared to live in the same manner as the residents.

Age 20+

Qualifications Experience not essential, but an advantage. All nationalities considered. Good command of English necessary.

Length of service 1 year minimum, if possible.

Terms Board, lodging and a small amount of pocket money provided; 1 day off per week.

When to apply Recruitment all year.

Publications Annual Report; *CVT News* regular magazine; information booklet.

THE CARR-GOMM SOCIETY LTD

Address 38 Gomm Road, Bermondsey, London SE16 2TX Tel 01-231 9284

Contact The Secretary

Organisation Founded in 1965, a charitable housing association whose purpose is to help the lonely and those who may become lonely, and to create neighbourhoods in which the experience of loneliness is less common and less painful.
Provides small, permanent houses for single people of either sex, all ages and any background, in which there is unintrusive domestic, social and spiritual support and encouragement to residents and neighbours to enter into the life of the wider community. Nationwide, the Society initiates and assists the establishment of autonomous local societies.

Opportunities A limited number of volunteers are needed to work and provide additional social support in the houses run by the Society in London. Residents have their own rooms, go out to work and lead their own lives, and work involves befriending them, giving practical help by accompanying them to appointments and making telephone calls, organising and participating in residents' activities, ranging from parties to group holidays, office duties, and being part of the staff team.

Personal qualities Applicants should be flexible with a general interest in personal welfare and a genuine commitment to working with lonely people.

Age 18+

Qualifications Previous voluntary experience useful but not essential. All nationalities considered. **HVC**

Length of service 4 months minimum.

Terms Single room accommodation with shared cooking facilities, £31.50 per week pocket money, food money, insurance, and travel pass provided. 40 hour week.

Briefing Volunteers are encouraged to participate in an induction course. Final assessment session during the last week of work can help with debriefing.

When to apply Recruitment all year.

Publications *Link* magazine; *Push on the Door* autobiography of Richard Carr-Gomm, founder of the Society.

CECIL HOUSES (INC)

Address 2 Priory Road, Kew, Richmond, Surrey TW9 3DG Tel 01-940 9828

Contact The General Manager and Secretary

Organisation A housing association charity founded in 1926, providing hostels for homeless and rootless women in central London, a sheltered hostel for active pensioners in Ealing and a residential care home for the frail elderly in Kew. It aims to create caring communities where individuals can mix with others in like circumstances, where they are offered food, warmth and comfort and where, above all else, they can have a sense of belonging.

Opportunities A limited number of volunteers are needed to help care for elderly residents and homeless women. Work includes driving the minibus to take residents shopping and to out-patients appointments; running the mobile shop; helping in the head office; and generally improving the residents' lifestyle.

Personal qualities Volunteers must be hard working, conscientious and enthusiastic and should be able to demonstrate charity, care and compassion.

Age 18+

Qualifications No qualifications or direct experience required. All nationalities considered. Working knowledge of English needed.

Length of service 1 month minimum; no maximum.

Terms Shared hostel accommodation, all meals, £14.50 per week pocket money and, after a set period of work, clothing allowance provided. 39 hour week.

When to apply Recruitment all year.

Publications Annual Report; information sheet.

COMMUNITY SERVICE VOLUNTEERS

Address 237 Pentonville Road, London N1 9NJ Tel 01-278 6601

Contact The Executive Director; applications from outside the UK to the Overseas Volunteer Programme Executive Director.

Organisation The national volunteer agency, a charity founded in 1962 to give all young people the chance to help others and to develop new ways of tackling social problems. Believing that everyone has something to offer and should have the chance to help, it has always operated a 'non-rejection' policy: everyone who wants to become a volunteer can. In addition to its volunteer programmes it operates the Advisory Service, promoting community action in education through publications, projects and training; Media Projects working with TV and radio companies on a range of social action broadcasts and helping voluntary community groups to use the local media; and the Youth Employment Schemes involving young unemployed people in work of community benefit and training.

Opportunities All the service opportunities rely on personal contact; many of them involve work with young people who need special care, the physically and mentally handicapped, the elderly and the homeless in community and health-related projects.

Current projects in homes and institutions include assisting in the work of tenants' associations, community groups and centres; acting as an older brother/sister to children who cannot for some reason live with their parents; arranging outings and activities for patients in psychiatric hospitals; involving those in youth custody centres in local community service; looking after young children in nurseries; sharing interests and activities with old people in residential homes; and extending the leisure opportunities of physically and mentally handicapped children in residential schools by helping teachers with swimming and other therapeutic programmes.

Placements in hostels, half-way houses and small group homes involve offering help and support to ex-prisoners in probation and after-care hostels; caring for single homeless people with drink problems; and helping mentally handicapped people leaving hospital to adapt to life in the community. Volunteers are placed in the community, developing special projects with social workers in area teams; and helping people with mental or physical handicaps to develop skills in training centres.

The Independent Living Scheme matches volunteers with individuals and families needing a high level of support to enable them to live in their own home instead of an institution, including physically disabled, elderly and mentally handicapped people, families needing practical help to stay together, children and young people with special needs, and the terminally ill.

The Health Services Programme places volunteers in hospitals and other health settings to provide an extra, complementary resource. Without trespassing on the distinctive professional roles of doctors, nurses, health visitors or social workers, they enable new or different approaches to be tried to help people lead full and healthy lives.

continued overleaf

Other schemes tailored to volunteers' special circumstances include local or away from home community service projects for people with physical disabilities, and special programmes for young offenders, young people in care and homeless young people in Greater London. Recruits 2000 volunteers annually, 150 of which are from overseas.

Personal qualities Applicants should have enthusiasm, energy, a commitment to helping others in the community and a desire to develop their potential.

Age 16-35, average 18-22; overseas volunteers 18+

Qualifications No academic qualifications or previous experience necessary. All nationalities considered. Good working knowledge of English essential. **HVC**

Length of service 4-12 months; 6 months minimum on the Independent Living Scheme.

Terms Volunteers are normally placed on projects away from their home area. Full board and accommodation, personal liability insurance, return travel within the UK and £14.50 per week pocket money provided. 35-40 hour week. One day off per week, but work may involve weekends and unsocial hours. One week's paid holiday and return fare after every four months of service. Overseas volunteers pay £310 placement fee.

Briefing Volunteers are consulted and briefed before their placement, which is subject to review after one month. Every effort is made to ensure that applicants are carefully matched to meet the requirements of the people they will be working with.
CSV staff liaise with volunteers and project organisers throughout the service. All volunteers are given the opportunity to comment on the placement at the end of their service.

When to apply Recruitment all year; volunteers are especially needed to start in spring and summer.

Publications *School and Community* termle magazine; community resource packs, simulation games, pupil work books, reports, audio visual materials and information leaflets.

THE CORRYMEELA COMMUNITY

Address Ballycastle, County Antrim, Northern Ireland Tel Ballycastle 62626

Contact The Volunteer Coordinator

Organisation Founded in 1965, Corrymeela is an open village situated on the north Antrim coast, comprising a house, cottages and youth village, and supported by the Corrymeela Community, a group of people drawn from many different Christian traditions who work for reconciliation in Northern Ireland in many different conflict situations and promote a concern for issues of peace and justice in the wider world. People under stress, such as those from problem areas, families of prisoners, the disabled and many others, go to Corrymeela for a break or holiday; conferences and other activities challenge participants to look critically at contemporary issues.

Opportunities A limited number of volunteers are needed to participate in the programme work of the residential centre, working with the groups who use the centre and being the link during their stay. They should expect to be involved in the practical aspects of running the establishment, assisting with catering arrangements, preparing accommodation, and working in the kitchen, laundry or reception. For short-term opportunities see *Working Holidays*.

Personal qualities Applicants must be fit and adaptable to cope with the demands and pressures of community life and a very busy programme, and have a commitment to the process of reconciliation.

Age 19+

Qualifications No qualifications or experience necessary. All nationalities considered.

Length of service 1 year, starting September.

Terms Accommodation in private study bedroom with all meals, £12 per week pocket money and insurance provided. Travel grant of £75 for volunteers from outside Ireland. 40-60 hour week. 6 days free per month; 1 week's holiday for every 3 months service.

Briefing Prospective volunteers should spend a few days at Corrymeela before applying. Compulsory 2 week orientation course. Weekly briefing and reflection programme with the full-time volunteer coordinator. Great care is taken in terms of staff support, external consultancy and pastoral access.

When to apply In time for September placement.

Publications *Corrymeela*; *Take Away This Hate*; general information leaflets.

FLYSHEET CAMPS SCOTLAND

Address Finniegill Childrens Farm, Lockerbie, Dumfriesshire, Scotland
Tel Boreland 211

Contact The Resident Organiser

Organisation An educational and recreational charity, founded in 1980 to provide a setting where people of all ages and backgrounds can experience living and working together in ways that are completely different from their everyday life, and thereby learn something about themselves and others that can be of value. Emphasis is placed on the concept of self-training, learning by doing something yourself, where the experience is as important as the end product. The remote farmstead high in the Moffat hills provides community children's camps which are run on the lines pioneered by Forest School Camps in the 1950s. There is an organic vegetable garden and a children's farm which is being developed as an approved Rare Breeds Survival Centre.

Opportunities A limited number of volunteers are needed to involve themselves totally with the work including caring for children and young people on Easter and summer camps, and helping to develop and maintain the stock of rare breeds of farm animals.
Self-organised wilderness project workcamps involve such activities as constructing and renovating buildings, repairing drystone walls and creating adventure playgrounds. Applicants should be aware that they may experience culture shock as the facilities are very primitive, there is no electricity and it is very isolated.

Personal qualities Above all else, a willingness to accept the unexpected in an unstructured setting is essential.

Age 16+

Qualifications No qualifications or experience necessary.
All nationalities considered. Basic English required. **HVC**

Length of service 4-6 months following an initial period of 2/3 weeks when both sides decide if they like each other.

Terms Very basic self-catering accommodation and insurance provided.
Volunteers share food cost, approx £2 per week.

Briefing Short training sessions arranged on child care for those helping with children's camps; plus sessions on seasonal activities such as tree planting, woodcraft skills, haymaking, fruit pickling, basic sheep shearing and spinning.

When to apply Recruitment all year.

Publications Information leaflet.

THE GIRL GUIDES ASSOCIATION (UK)

Address 17-19 Buckingham Palace Road, London SW1W OPT
Tel 01-834 6242

Contact The Secretary

Organisation Founded in 1910, the Association aims to provide a
programme embracing a wide range of leisure-time activities and
interests which, while enjoyable in themselves, have an underlying
educational purpose, namely, to develop individual character based on
the values expressed in the Promise and Law.

Opportunities Volunteer work is available at some of the Girl Guide
Training Centres. Projects may include training adult leaders, or
administration duties in connection with Guide Houses. The work is
sometimes strenuous with long hours, but is valuable and rewarding.

Personal qualities These are determined by the Guider-in-Charge for
each centre.

Age 18+

Qualifications Qualifications and experience required vary according to
the position. Volunteers must be members of the Association. **HVC**

Length of service Variable.

Terms Board, accommodation and pocket money provision vary
according to the position. Insurance provided in some cases.
Travel costs usually paid by the volunteer. Advice given to participants on
obtaining sponsorship. Members are encouraged to write articles for the
magazines once they have completed their assignments.

Publications *The Brownie*; *Today's Guide*; *Guiding* magazines.

THE GLENCREE CENTRE FOR RECONCILIATION AND PEACE

Address Glencree, near Bray, Eniskerry, County Wicklow, Ireland Tel Dublin 86 09 62

Contact The Centre Coordinator

Organisation Founded in 1974 the Centre works to discover and promote the conditions for a just and peaceful society. A spirit of Christian commitment to this ideal inspired its foundation and continues to motivate its varied activities of peace making and training, North/South youth exchanges, farm education programmes for junior schools, seminars, conferences, workcamps and the respectful use of natural resources. The Centre consists of a farm of 30 acres, a large organic vegetable garden and extensive buildings, and welcomes victims of violence and people from divided communities and areas of conflict for a period of rest and recreation.

Opportunities A limited number of long-term volunteers are needed to work on the farm, on general maintenance, in the garden, household or office. In addition they assist staff in all programmes, for example those working on the farm also teach how to milk cows and care for livestock as part of the farm education programme. For short-term opportunities see *Working Holidays*.

Personal qualities Volunteers should have a commitment to, as well as an acceptance of, the work. A willingness to learn is essential, and they should also have a desire to live and grow in community life together with an ability to change their attitudes in order to create an atmosphere of dignity and mutual respect.

Age 20+

Qualifications Experience necessary for farm, garden and office work. All nationalities may apply; EC nationals preferred. Good working knowledge of English required.

Length of service 1 year from September, which may be extended by an extra year.

Terms Accommodation in individual rooms in volunteers' house, meals at the Centre and insurance provided, but no travel costs. EC nationals on long-term service receive government unemployment assistance of IR£29.95 per week.

Briefing Prospective volunteers are encouraged to stay at the Centre for a minimum of 2 weeks prior to being considered for a position. Compulsory 2 week orientation course in September.

When to apply Apply by end June; earlier application preferred.

Publication *Glencree News* bi-monthly newsletter; information leaflets.

GREAT GEORGES PROJECT

Address The Blackie, Great George Street, Liverpool 1 Tel Liverpool 709 5109

Contact The Duty Officer

Organisation Founded in 1968, the Great Georges Community Cultural Project, known locally as The Blackie, is a centre for experimental work in the arts, sports, games and education of today. Housed in a former church in an area typical of the modern inner-city - multi-racial, relatively poor, with a high crime rate and a high energy level; sometimes a lot of fun. The Project sets about its task of building bridges between the artist and the community with great enthusiasm, offering a wide range of cultural programmes, workshops and exhibitions including pottery, sculpture, printing, film/video making, photography, painting, writing, outdoor plays, carpentry, puppetry, playstructures, music, mime and dance. Open 7 days a week, 10.00-24.00.

Opportunities Volunteers are needed to work with children/adults in projects undertaken at The Blackie and in the local community, with endless opportunities to learn and create.
The general work of running the Project is shared as fairly as possible with everyone doing some administration, cleaning, talking to visitors and playing games with the children. Recruits 100-150 volunteers annually.

Personal qualities Applicants should have a good sense of humour, stamina, a readiness to learn, and a willingness to work hard and to share any skills they may have. The children/young people who visit the Project are tough, intelligent, friendly and regard newcomers as a fair target for jokes, so the ability to exert discipline without being authoritarian is essential.

Age 18+

Qualifications No direct experience required. All nationalities considered. Good working knowledge of English required.

Length of service Minimum 1 month, no maximum. Volunteers are particularly needed at Christmas, Easter and summer.

Terms Accommodation in shared rooms at staff house; long-term volunteers may have own room. Vegetarian breakfast and evening meal provided, cooking on a rota basis. Those who can afford to, contribute approx £10 per week to cover food and housekeeping. Wages generally paid after 6 months. 12 hour day minimum, 6 day week.

Briefing Orientation course includes a talk with films and a pack of Project literature.

When to apply Recruitment all year.

Publications Information leaflet for volunteers and numerous pamphlets.

GREEN DESERTS LTD

Address Rougham, Bury St Edmunds, Suffolk IP30 9LY Tel Beyton 70265

Contact The Company Secretary

Organisation A charity founded in 1976, Green Deserts promotes desert reclamation in arid zones of the world, working for the permanent relief of famine through community forestry in action, forestry farming and appropriate technology. Equally concerned with working towards a sustainable existence at home, it sponsors an organic market garden and tree nursery to supply saplings for planting on community programme projects in Suffolk.

Opportunities A limited number of volunteers are needed to provide fundraising and administrative support; there are also some vacancies for farmers, gardeners, tree surgeons and other experts in forestry and agriculture.

Personal qualities Applicants should be committed to the aims and methods of the organisation and, where appropriate, have a willingness to pass on their skills.

Age 18+

Qualifications Qualifications needed vary according to the task. Previous experience useful, but training can be given. All nationalities considered. **HVC**

Length of service Negotiable; usually 3+ months.

Terms Accommodation and vegetarian catering provided. Volunteers are expected to provide their own pocket money and travel costs.

When to apply Recruitment all year.

Publications *Green Deserts* regular magazine.

HOTHORPE HALL

Address Christian Conference Centre, Theddingworth, near Lutterworth, Leicester LE17 6QX Tel Market Harborough 880257

Contact The Director

Organisation Founded in 1955 and formerly known as the Lutheran Centre, Hothorpe Hall provides conference facilities for groups of up to 120 people, of many different denominations and backgrounds but mainly from churches and schools.

Opportunities Volunteers are needed to look after the guests and maintain the facilities. Posts are available as kitchen/domestic assistants, servers, gardeners and maintenance assistants. Participation in communal worship, devotions and discussions is expected. Recruits up to 20 volunteers annually.

Personal qualities Applicants should have a Christian commitment and a willingness to join in as a member of the community, and be in good physical health.

Age 17+

Qualifications No academic qualifications or direct experience needed, but specific skills in such areas as art, music and gardening enable the volunteer to make a valuable and interesting contribution to community life. All nationalities considered. Good spoken English required.

Length of service 6 weeks-1 year.

Terms Shared accommodation, all meals, accident insurance, and staffroom provided. Pocket money of £5 per week for the first six weeks, £10 per week thereafter. Participants pay own travel expenses. 40 hour week.

When to apply Recruitment all year; volunteers needed especially in the summer.

THE LADYPOOL PROJECT

Address 112 Whitecroft Road, Sheldon, Birmingham B26 3RG
Tel 021-743 3649

Contact The Honorary Secretary

Organisation Founded in 1981, an evangelical Christian charity engaged in general social work and providing boating activities for physically and especially mentally handicapped people. Working with the charity Youth Afloat it operates several narrowboats on and around the canals of the West Midlands, providing outing and holiday facilities for handicapped and disadvantaged groups. Other activities include a prayer and visiting service for the seriously ill, offshore summer sailing camps for the handicapped at Dartmouth, and Open Christmas, when food, shelter and a change of clothes are provided for approx 700 tramps, lonely folk and social misfits whilst most of the government's social service centres are closed.

Opportunities A limited number of volunteers are needed to crew the narrowboats and help out as required on the Project's activities in Birmingham and the West Midlands.

Personal qualities Applicants should have a willingness to work and cooperate; a Christian commitment is preferred.

Age 17+

Qualifications Experience with the mentally handicapped useful, but not essential. Applicants must be able to swim and boating experience is useful. All nationalities considered. Knowledge of English required. **HVC**

Length of service From a few days to a few years.

Terms Short-term accommodation provided on boats, with full kitchen facilities; longer term housing can be arranged.
Volunteers contribute approx £5 per week towards food. Accident insurance and local travel expenses provided. Sponsorship encouraged.

Briefing Compulsory 2 day visit prior to appointment to ensure that applicants are compatible with the Project.

When to apply Recruitment all year.

Publication *Ladypool Project News* occasional newsletter.

LAND USE VOLUNTEERS

Address Horticultural Therapy, Goulds Ground, Vallis Way, Frome, Somerset BA11 3DW Tel Frome 64782

Contact The Head of the Volunteer Unit

Organisation The Society for Horticultural Therapy is a non-profitmaking company founded in 1978 to help disabled and handicapped people enjoy and benefit from gardening, horticulture and agriculture. Land Use Volunteers, its volunteer service, began in 1981 and is one of a wide range of practical services offered to disabled people and those who work with them.

Opportunities Volunteers are needed to work throughout the country with handicapped, disabled and disadvantaged people, living and working on rehabilitation projects on the basis of a common interest in plants and animals to enable land use activities work more effectively. Projects in the past have included developing a small hospital market garden whilst working with psychiatric patients and care staff; working with adult mentally handicapped residents at a home farm trust, breeding rare domestic animals and organic growing; training clients and other care staff in simple horticultural tasks; and working with ex-drug addicts and offenders in planting and gardening. Also work with the physically handicapped, hearing impaired, the blind, elderly and disturbed young people. Approx 30 volunteers are on projects at any one time.

Personal qualities Applicants must be self-confident, adaptable, able to fit into a small community with a desire to transmit their special land use skills.

Age 18+

Qualifications Volunteers should have qualifications, skills and/or basic experience in agriculture, horticulture or forestry.
All nationalities considered. Knowledge of English required. **HVC**

Length of service 3-12 months.

Terms Full board and lodging on site, £15 per week pocket money and travel expenses provided. One week's leave and return fare for every 4 months completed service. Applicants must be available for interview in the UK. 40 hour week.

When to apply Recruitment all year.

Publication *Growth Point* quarterly magazine.

LANGLEY HOUSE TRUST

Address 46 Market Square, Witney, Oxfordshire OX8 6AL Tel Witney 74075

Contact The General Secretary

Organisation Founded in 1958, the aim of the Trust is to spread and sustain Christianity among ex-offenders. It has 13 residential family homes in England for homeless ex-offenders, cared for by full-time staff drawn from all Christian denominations. Through the provision of half-way homes, sheltered working communities, retirement homes and a drug rehabilitation home it gives each man a breathing space in his life in a caring, supportive environment, so that he may perhaps recuperate, take stock, replan his life and be rehabilitated back into society.

Opportunities A limited number of volunteers are needed in sheltered working communities in Hampshire, Somerset and Leicestershire, to assist with domestic duties and work alongside the residents in workshops or on horticultural and gardening activities.

Personal qualities Applicants should be practising Christians, mature, spiritually, mentally and physically strong to enable them to cope with the demands of working alongside and empathising with the homeless male ex-offender, with commonsense and a sense of humour.

Age 18+

Qualifications No qualifications or previous experience necessary. British nationals only due to the necessity of fully understanding the background circumstances of the residents.

Length of service 4-12 months.

Terms Volunteers receive comfortable, single room accommodation with main meals taken with the resident family and staff, £13.75 per week pocket money, insurance and travel costs.
35-40 hour week.

Briefing Experiences may be freely discussed with staff as an informal debriefing service.

When to apply Recruitment all year.

Publications Newsletter, six monthly; prayer letter, quarterly.

THE LEONARD CHESHIRE FOUNDATION

Address Leonard Cheshire House, 26-29 Maunsel Street, London SW1P 2QN Tel 01-828 1822

Contact The Secretary to the Personnel Adviser

Organisation A charitable trust founded in 1948, with nearly 200 homes in 36 countries including 75 in the UK. It has no boundaries of sex, creed or race, concerned only with the care of severely handicapped people. The common aim of all Cheshire Homes is to provide care and shelter in an atmosphere as close as possible to that of a family home; residents are encouraged to take whatever part they can in the running of the Home and to participate in decisions affecting it. The Family Support Services scheme provides part-time care attendants to help prevent or alleviate stress in families with a handicapped member and enables disabled people to continue living at home.

Opportunities Care assistant volunteers are needed in many Homes in Great Britain, to enable residents to live as active and productive a life as possible. They assist with the general care of residents who require help in personal matters, including washing, dressing and feeding, as well as with hobbies, letter writing and other recreational activities. Volunteers may also do domestic work, gardening or decorating. Recruits 70-80 volunteers annually.

Personal qualities Applicants must have an interest in and a desire to help the handicapped; the work is hard and requires understanding and dedication.

Age 18+

Qualifications Previous experience useful but not essential. Preference is often given to those planning a future career in social work or in the medical field. All nationalities considered. Good working knowledge of English essential.

Length of service 3-12 months.

Terms Shared accommodation, meals, a minimum of £14.50 per week pocket money, and personal liability insurance provided. Volunteers pay their travel costs. Up to 39 hour, 4 day week.

Briefing No orientation course given; volunteers are under direct supervision of Head of Care at the Home concerned.

When to apply Apply mainly for summer but jobs may become available at any time of the year.

Publications Annual Report; *How the Cheshire Homes Started* booklet outlining the Foundations's history; information booklets and leaflets.

THE MISSIONS TO SEAMEN

Address St Michael Paternoster Royal, College Hill, London EC4R 2RL
Tel 01-248 5202

Contact The Secretary to The Assistant General Secretary

Organisation An Anglican missionary society founded in 1856, caring for
the spiritual, material and moral welfare of seafarers around the globe.
The Missions help to combat isolation, exploitation and the dangers of the
sea, working for improvements in conditions, education and welfare,
serving seafarers of every race, colour and creed, offering a ministry of
word, sacrament, counselling care and Christian welcome. The most
important feature is the visit of the chaplain and staff to each ship on
arrival in port.

Opportunities There are volunteer service schemes for student
assistants, providing an opportunity to be involved in practical Christian
service within the shipping industry. Work is varied and involves visiting
ships, conducting sightseeing tours, arranging sporting events, visiting
hospitals, and helping with worship. Serving in the seafarers' centres can
include bar and shop work, arranging video shows, telephone calls,
gardening and cleaning. Recruits approx 24 volunteers annually.

Personal qualities Applicants should be sympathetic and understanding,
good at quickly establishing relationships, prepared to befriend people of
all nationalities and must have an interest in this particular form of
ministry.

Age 18-24

Qualifications No specific experience necessary, but the ability to swim
and possession of a clean driving licence are required. Applicants must
be communicant members of the Church of England and need three
suitable references.

Length of service 1 year, starting September.

Terms Board and lodging, travel costs, medical/accident insurance, £14
per week pocket money and 3 weeks holiday per year provided.

Briefing Weekend training session arranged.

When to apply As soon as possible.

Publications Two newspapers *Flying Angel News* and *The Sea. Prayer
Union* booklet provides details on ports and personnel.

NATIONAL COUNCIL OF YMCAS

Address 640 Forest Road, London E17 3DZ Tel 01-520 5599

Contact The Head of the Education & Programme Development Department

Organisation A charity founded in 1844, which works with young people from all walks of life to encourage them to live full and worthwhile lives and develop their potential, to show them that alongside love, care and understanding there exists a hope for the future which is manifested in the life of Jesus Christ. The YMCA is part of a worldwide movement of over 26 million members in 96 countries across the world, and runs over 250 outdoor pursuit centres, hostels and youth centres throughout the UK.

Opportunities Volunteers are needed to assist in the whole range of the Council's activities, including helping at local centres with basic administration and reception work; working with young children in playgroups; helping in youth clubs and programmes for the young unemployed; and organising activities in outdoor pursuit centres. Many of these opportunities are particularly useful for applicants intending to gain some grass roots experience prior to entering teaching or youth and social work. Recruits an average of 50 volunteers annually.

Personal qualities Applicants should demonstrate a willingness to give, patience and understanding. A mature, responsible approach is required for posts at outdoor pursuit centres.

Age 18+

Qualifications Previous experience not required for most of the posts; relevant skills and experience essential for posts at the outdoor pursuit centres. All nationalities considered. **HVC**

Length of service Usually 1 year.

Terms Accommodation provided where necessary. Volunteers receive pocket money, insurance and travel within the UK.

When to apply Recruitment all year.

Publications Annual Review.

NATIONAL CYRENIANS

Address 13 Wincheap, Canterbury, Kent CT1 3TB Tel Canterbury 451641

Contact The Volunteers Secretary

Organisation Founded in 1970 with the aims of running experimental projects for homeless single people and acting as a campaigning body for their needs. There are now over 100,000 homeless in Britain, who have fallen through the safety net of the welfare state. Affiliated groups in 26 towns run day centres, night shelters and residential houses for single homeless people, particularly those who seek a supportive environment in the form of group living. The groups believe that residents should be accepted as they are, rather than as society would like them to be, and that the homes should consist of small sharing groups, run democratically with everyone sharing decisions.

Opportunities Volunteers work in teams of 2-4 per project, and lead the house, helping the group to take collective responsibility on house affairs thus enabling residents to do more for themselves; emphasis is on the sharing of chores and authority. Work involves collecting rents, distributing medicines and liaising with agencies on behalf of residents; other tasks include working out arrangements for cooking, cleaning and shopping, ensuring that decisions are reached within the house to deal with problems that arise, maintaining house rules and creating a reasonable stable and homely atmosphere. The work is often difficult, especially if there is a high turnover of people. Recruits approx 250 volunteers annually.

Personal qualities Applicants should have a caring attitude, able to live and work with fellow volunteers and help weld the group together and build the community. They must be able to cope with the demanding physical and emotional pressures of community living, and have the confidence to take responsibility.

Age 18-30

Qualifications No qualifications or experience necessary. All nationalities considered. Fluent English required.

Length of service 6-12 months

Terms Volunteers receive own room and board, travel within the UK and a minimum £23 per week pocket money. 1 free day per week; 1 week's leave every 3 months.

Briefing Successful applicants accepted initially for 1 month trial period. Regular meetings held to share experience and discuss any problems.

When to apply Recruitment all year.

Publications *Women and Homelessness* report; *The Unfairest Game in Town* young homelessness report; *Homelessness - Filling a Need* booklet; information leaflets.

THE NORTH DEVON HOLIDAY HOME TRUST FOR DEPRIVED CHILDREN

Address Alswear, South Molton, North Devon EX36 4LH Tel Bishops Nympton 244

Contact The Director of the Trust

Organisation A charity founded in 1969 to provide holidays in a farm environment for deprived children from industrial areas and major cities of Britain. Most of the children are aged 7-11 and in real need of care and attention, having been referred by social and welfare agencies; they stay at the Trust's smallholding which comprises Hobby Horse Farm, village stores and several cottages. It runs a self-sufficiency programme, growing its own fruit, herbs and vegetables, keeping animals and carrying out woodcraft; the emphasis is on simplicity and there is a friendly non-institutional atmosphere.

Opportunities Long-term volunteers are required to help run the farm, carry out maintenance or repair work and help with domestic duties. Volunteers able to work for the entire summer programme are needed for farm, office and domestic work, and to supervise and play with the children, including raft, bridge and dam building, nature walks, pottery, origami, donkey rides and outings to the seaside and local moors. Recruits 40 volunteers annually, 30 for the summer programme.

Personal qualities Applicants should have a desire to contribute something to society and a willingness to work hard and well without too much supervision. A certain maturity is required as volunteers can expect from the children unwillingness to join in, stealing, fighting, lying, cheating and foul language.

Age 16+

Qualifications No qualifications or experience necessary. All nationalities considered, but good English is required.

Length of service 1 month minimum, no maximum; summer programme of 8 weeks, mid July-September.

Terms Full board and basic cottage accommodation provided; long-term volunteers have own room. Volunteers pay their travel costs. 35-40 hour week.

Briefing The first week of the summer programme is a training week.

When to apply Recruitment all year.

Publications Information leaflets.

THE OCKENDEN VENTURE

Address Ockenden, Guildford Road, Woking, Surrey GU22 7UU
Tel Woking 72012

Contact The Recruitment Secretary

Organisation A charity founded in 1955, providing home, health and
education at home and abroad for stateless refugees and casualties of
conflict and oppression, especially children.
The scale of the problem is such that, despite enormous international
resettlement programmes, there are still over 10 million unsettled
refugees throughout the world, increasing numbers of whom are unable to
find asylum anywhere. As well as concern for child rescue at international
level and refugee resettlement, the Venture also provides intermediate
treatment for young offenders, education, care and rehabilitation for
children who are deprived, at risk or in trouble, and long-term care for
young handicapped refugees.

Opportunities Volunteers are needed in the Venture's UK homes to work
as general assistants with refugee families and children, and with mentally
and/or physically handicapped children/young people, many of whom
are refugees. Help is required with gardening, cooking, painting,
maintenance and creative activities. Longer term volunteers are required
for refugee reception centres. There are very limited opportunities for
field work with refugees in Sudan, Pakistan and Thailand.

Personal qualities Applicants should have a genuine desire to help, a
willingness to work hard, and be physically fit. The houses are run on non-
institutional lines in order to create homes, so volunteers are expected to
accept a fair share of responsibility at all levels for child care and
domestic work.

Age 18+

Qualifications Qualifications or experience not generally necessary. EC
nationals only. Fluent English essential.

Length of service 6 months minimum, preferably 1 year.

Terms Volunteers receive full board and lodging, employer's liability
insurance and a minimum of £10 per week pocket money, increasing after
a trial period to around £20. 5-6 day week.
Four weeks holiday per year, pro rata for shorter periods.

When to apply Recruitment all year; most volunteers join in
August/September.

Publications Annual Report.

PARADISE HOUSE ASSOCIATION

Address Paradise House, Painswick, Stroud, Gloucestershire GL6 6TN
Tel Painswick 813276

Contact The Principal

Organisation Founded in 1976 as a registered charity, Paradise House
provides training, home care and employment for mentally handicapped
adolescents and young adults, based on the well-tried principles and
practices derived from the insights of Rudolf Steiner. All the activities are
directed towards providing an environment and a human climate in which
each resident can discover and develop their own potential.

Opportunities Volunteers are needed to help look after small groups of
mentally handicapped people in a family atmosphere, to train them to do
useful, meaningful tasks, look after their needs and give them the
education and opportunities they require and deserve. Participants assist
in the running of craft workshops, classes, the house, garden and farm,
and the provision of leisure activities. Recruits approx 12 volunteers
annually.

Personal qualities Applicants should have an interest in helping
handicapped people, be willing to work hard and enjoy community living.

Age 18+; older people preferred.

Qualifications No academic qualifications or experience necessary. All
nationalities considered. The ability to communicate in English is
essential.

Length of service 1 year minimum.

Terms Accommodation in single or shared rooms, all meals, £12.50 per
week pocket money, £240 annual holiday contribution and insurance
provided. One free period a day, one free day a week. Motor scooter
available for personal use.

Briefing Introductory course on arrival.

When to apply Recruitment all year.

Publications Information leaflets.

RETIRED EXECUTIVES ACTION CLEARING-HOUSE

Address 89 Southwark Street, London SE1 0HD Tel 01-928 0452

Contact The Director

Organisation A non-profitmaking charity founded in 1979 by a small group of executives from the business and voluntary sectors, who reasoned that retirement should be looked upon as the beginning of a new way of life and the chance of continuing to be active in the community, and were concerned that the potential resources of retired professionals from business and industry were not being deployed to advantage. It promotes the provision of voluntary assistance to community groups, voluntary organisations and charities by retired executives with professional skills. Although it is willing to help to define problems and develop proposals in assessing the resources that are required, REACH does not initiate projects on its own.

Opportunities Retired executives are matched to charitable organisations which must prove that there is a genuine need for the volunteer's skills which cannot be met in any other way, and that the task makes full use of the business or professional skills requested. Skills in high demand include budgeting, management, marketing and public relations. In addition to placements in conventional voluntary organisations, there are also opportunities in the fields of arts, culture, environment, religion and sport.

Personal qualities Applicants should have a desire to utilise their skills for the benefit of the community and a willingness to adapt to unfamiliar circumstances.

Age No restrictions

Qualifications Volunteers bring skills and experience gained during their working lives. **HVC**

Length of service No limit

When to apply Recruitment all year.

Terms Applicants should state their skills, the duration and amount of time they are willing to give, and any geographical constraints. Work can be full or part time; most volunteers work from home so board and accommodation is not usually provided although expenses are paid.

Publications *Work After Work* a guide to life after retirement; Annual Report; information leaflets.

THE RICHMOND FELLOWSHIP

Address 8 Addison Road, London W14 8DL Tel 01-603 6373

Contact The Personnel Officer

Organisation A charity founded in 1959 with the principal aim of promoting better understanding of human relations, in particular those factors which tend to foster mental health or lead to emotional disturbance. Carries out a programme of education based on and linked with a therapeutic programme, bringing together people who have suffered emotional distress and people of the area who are concerned to assist in bringing about integration and mutually rewarding relationships. The Fellowship run over 40 halfway houses in the UK for children, adolescents, young people, families, older people, those diagnosed as schizophrenic, recovering alcoholics, ex-drug users, and people needing minimal support. Also provides training courses and a consultative service.

Opportunities Volunteers are needed to work with the emotionally disturbed in residential and day care centres, and in addition to helping with the practical necessities of life, are involved in activities which include gardening, cooking, art, music, woodwork, decoration and drama groups, sport and relaxation. There are also opportunities for administrative workers.

Personal qualities Applicants should have the commitment to do a very difficult and demanding but rewarding job, and the ability to relate sensitively and sensibly to the residents.

Age 21 +

Qualifications Applicants should have some experience with the emotionally disturbed and of field/residential social work.
Skills in recreational activities an advantage. All nationalities considered. Fluent English required.

Length of service 6 months minimum; preferably 1 year.

Terms Volunteers are expected to accept the obligations and responsibilities which apply to staff members, including professional relationship with residents, responsibility within the structure, punctuality and codes of practice. Board, lodging and accident insurance provided. Pocket money £15 per week for 6 months service; £20 per week for 1 year's service. 6 day, 48 hour week. 26 days annual leave, pro rata for shorter terms of service.

Briefing Volunteers undergo an induction course on entering a programme. The leaving process is carefully planned as much for the sake of residents as for the volunteer.

When to apply Recruitment all year.

Publications Annual Report; *Mental Health and the Community: Report of the Richmond Fellowship Enquiry, 1983.*

THE SIMON COMMUNITY

Address St Joseph's House, 129 Malden Road, London NW5 4HS
Tel 01-485 6639

Contact The Deputy Community Leader

Organisation Founded in 1963, the Community is the mission of caring on skidrow, committed to caring and campaigning for and with the homeless, rootless and all of no fixed abode. Catholic founded and inspired, aiming to put into practice the simple Gospel message, but completely ecumenical in action with members of all faiths and none. Residents are men and women, young and old, who have been rejected by society and being without support from family or friends have slipped through the net of the welfare state, and for whom no other provision exists. A night shelter, community houses and a farmhouse comprise a tier system enabling residents to move from house to house and find the appropriate level of support at a particular point in time. A long-term caring, supportive environment is provided where the individual can regain self respect; for those who are temporarily homeless, there is provision for emergency stopover.

Opportunities Volunteers are needed to live and work with the residents of Community houses in London and, at the Community leaders' discretion, at the farmhouse in Kent. Activities include helping residents obtain medical care and social security, referral to other organisations, talking to the residents, sorting old clothes, cooking, fundraising and campaigning, housework, administration, group meetings, night duty, going to rough sleeping sites in London with tea, sandwiches and clothing to make contact with homeless people and helping at a night shelter. The work is emotionally demanding, dealing with problems including alcoholism, drug addiction and psychiatric disorders; workers and residents share in the chores and decision making. The experience is of particular interest to those seriously considering social work.

Personal qualities Applicants should have a commitment to, and some perception of, the aims and philosophy of the Community. They should have a willingness to learn and adapt, the ability to relate and respond to people, and must be caring, sensible, mature and stable enough to take the burden of other people's problems while retaining their own balance. Volunteers should be capable of taking initiatives within the framework of a team, learning to cope with crises. A sense of humour is an asset.

Age 18+; exceptions possible.

Qualifications Academic qualifications or experience not essential. EC nationals only. Good command of English necessary. **HVC**

Length of service 3 months minimum.

Terms Workers live alongside residents, sharing the same facilities, food and conditions; accommodation can be basic and rough. Pocket money £9.25 per week. Average 16 hour day; 1 day per week free.

When to apply Recruitment all year.

Publications *Simon Star* quarterly newsletter. Two books on the Community's work: *Caring on Skid Row*; *No Fixed Abode*; information leaflets.

SUE RYDER FOUNDATION

Address Sue Ryder Home, Cavendish, Suffolk CO10 8AY Tel Glemsford 280252

Contact The Administration Officer

Organisation A charity founded in 1952 with over 80 homes throughout the world, primarily for the disabled and incurable but also admitting those who, on discharge from hospital, still need care and attention. The aim is to provide residents with a family sense of being at home, each with something to contribute to the common good. Seeks to render personal service to those in need and to give affection to those who are unloved, regardless of age, race or creed. The homes are a living memorial to the millions who gave their lives during two world wars in defence of human values, and to the countless others who are suffering and dying today as a result of persecution.

Opportunities Volunteers are needed in 15 homes all over the UK. Work includes helping with patients, routine office work, assisting in the kitchen, garden, museum, coffee and gift shop at headquarters, general maintenance and other essential work arising. Experienced volunteers are also needed for secretarial work and nursing.

Personal qualities Applicants should be flexible and adaptable, with a keen interest in caring work.

Age 18+

Qualifications Qualifications or experience not essential, but an advantage; preference given to students or graduates.
Doctor's certificate required. All nationalities considered.
Good command of English required.

Length of service 2 months minimum.

Terms Board and lodging usually in double rooms and £4 per week pocket money provided. 35 hour week.

Briefing Two week trial period. Instruction provided at beginning of placement.

When to apply Recruitment all year; larger numbers of volunteers required in summer.

Publications *An outline of the Sue Ryder Foundation's work in Britain and abroad*; *Remembrance* annual news magazine.

THE TIME FOR GOD SCHEME

Address 2 Chester House, Pages Lane, London N10 1PR Tel 01-883 1504

Contact The Organiser

Organisation A charity founded in 1966 and sponsored by the Baptist Union, Church of England, United Reformed Church, Baptist Missionary Society and Methodist Association of Youth Clubs. It recruits for many organisations, enabling young people to give service to churches and the community and thereby grow in maturity and faith, and understand the task of the church, Christ's mission of love for all men.

Opportunities Volunteers are required to work in England and occasionally Wales, in churches and church-based community centres. Work involves typing, decorating, visiting and worship with play, study and youth groups; doing domestic chores, organising activities and outings, or just acting as good listeners in homes for disadvantaged children, the handicapped or the elderly; reception/ office duties, domestic chores and organising social activities in hostels, outdoor activity and rehabilitation centres. Recruits approx 60 volunteers annually.

Personal qualities Volunteers require the personal resources to enable them to benefit from and contribute to the scheme, and applicants should have concern for others, be willing to accept the challenge of Christian service and wish to be involved in God's work in the world. Volunteers should be be committed Christians or genuinely searching for Christian faith.

Age 17-25; overseas volunteers 18+

Qualifications Experience not necessary, but those with some skills and experience are easier to place. Volunteers must be recommended by a local church of any denomination. Up to 6 places for overseas volunteers. **HVC**

Length of service 3-12 months; 6 months minimum preferred, except during the summer. 6 months minimum for overseas volunteers.

Terms Full board and lodging in private house, staff quarters or self-catering flat, £13.75 per week pocket money and accident insurance provided. Return fares paid for exploratory visit and at the start, end and after every 3 months of service.
40 hour week; 1 week's leave after 6 months. UK volunteers: £5 registration fee and fare to interview up to a maximum of £7; overseas volunteers: £100 registration fee, travel and insurance costs.

Briefing Compulsory 2 day orientation conferences held twice yearly; most volunteers attend one before or soon after they start. Conference at the end of service can act as a debriefing session.

When to apply Apply 2-6 months in advance.

Publications Review of the Scheme, 1981-1984; information leaflets and brochures.

SECTION V

VOLUNTARY SERVICE IN THE UK+IRELAND
ADVISORY BODIES

NATIONAL COUNCIL FOR VOLUNTARY ORGANISATIONS

Address 26 Bedford Square, London WC1B 3HU Tel 01-636 4066

Organisation Founded in 1919 as the National Council of Social Service, it is the central voluntary agency for the maintenance and promotion of voluntary social action in the UK, having pioneered many of the present day services including Age Concern, Youth Hostels Association, Citizens Advice Bureaux and the Charities Aid Foundation. Its aims are to extend the involvement of voluntary organisations in responding to social issues; to be a resource centre for voluntary organisations; to protect the interests and independence of voluntary organisations and charities; to develop cooperation between them and statutory authorities; and to encourage international cooperation in voluntary and social service. Current areas of work include the effects of unemployment, adolescents in trouble or need, provision for ethnic minorities, inner city deprivation, community health initiatives and services in rural areas.
Through the provision of information, training, legal, financial, publishing and advisory services the NCVO assists voluntary organisations to develop their functions. Also has links with voluntary organisations in other countries and uses these to promote the exchange of information and experience, and to encourage the voluntary sector to develop an international dimension in its work.

Advice Provides current information on projects, policies, events, organisations, conferences and other news of importance to voluntary organisations. Has a large library and an enquiry and reference service.

Publications *Voluntary Action* regular magazine; *Voluntary Organisations* annual directory; *Citizens Advice Notes* specialist information on current legislation; *Employment Opportunities in the Voluntary Sector* information sheet; *Guide to NCVO Services*; wide range of titles covering voluntary action, social services and welfare, charities and voluntary organisations, community schemes, health, human rights, inner cities, media and race relations; Annual Report.

NORTHERN IRELAND COUNCIL FOR VOLUNTARY ACTION

Address 2 Annadale Avenue, Belfast BT7 3JR Tel Belfast 640011

Organisation Founded in 1938 as the Northern Ireland Council of Social Service, an independent organisation of charitable status with the broad aim of promoting the general good of the community in Northern Ireland. More specifically its objectives are to promote, support and facilitate voluntary action with emphasis on action aimed at socially deprived and disadvantaged individuals, families and communities; to provide a regional service of information, support and training to voluntary organisations; to identify, by itself or in cooperation with other bodies, community needs which can be met by voluntary organisations, and to develop projects to meet these needs; and to provide opportunities for voluntary organisations to consider matters of social concern, expressing their views on them to the government and other relevant bodies. Provides advice, services and grants for the voluntary sector; a community information bank stores information on social issues and developments.

Advice Provides advice on where to apply in Northern Ireland for voluntary opportunities and referral to relevant agencies.

Publications *Scope* magazine; *Index of Community Groups in Northern Ireland*; *Guide to Social Services*; *Poverty Pack*.

NATIONAL SOCIAL SERVICES BOARD

Address 71 Lower Leeson Street, Dublin 2 Tel Dublin 682422

Organisation Founded in 1971 as the National Social Services Council and funded by the Irish Department of Health, it has the main aims of providing information, resources and advice on social services to the public and the voluntary sectors. The Development Section provides back-up mainly to local voluntary organisations, by giving advice on such matters as insurance and employment, and by arranging training courses; the Information Section services local community information centres.

Publications *Relate* magazine outlining Irish social services; *Directory of National Voluntary Services* listing voluntary organisations in Ireland.

SCOTTISH COUNCIL FOR COMMUNITY AND VOLUNTARY ORGANISATIONS

Address 18-19 Claremont Crescent, Edinburgh EH7 4QD Tel 031-556 3882

Organisation Founded in 1943 as the Scottish Council of Social Service, an independent national council with the prime objective of promoting and supporting voluntary service and action throughout Scotland, enabling other voluntary organisations to be effective. It extends the range of voluntary endeavour, advocates particular issues, promotes and safeguards the values of voluntary endeavour and provides services to these ends.

Advice Information and referral services.

Publications *National Voluntary Organisations in Scotland* directory; *Third Sector* bi-monthly magazine; information packs; Annual Review.

THE VOLUNTEER CENTRE

Address 29 Lower King's Road, Berkhamsted, Hertfordshire HP4 2AB Tel Berkhamsted 73311

Organisation The national advisory agency on volunteer action and community involvement which speaks with an independent voice, aiming to foster dispassionate, and sometimes critical, debate on current volunteering practice. It promotes voluntary action within the statutory services, by voluntary organisations, self-help groups, or informally by individuals. It seeks to help projects involving unemployed people who volunteer, services 300 volunteer bureaux, acts as a link between the media and those involved in social action and undertakes training for volunteer organisers.

Advice Substantial library and information service.

Publications *Involve* magazine, 8 times per year; *Information Volunteered* quarterly journal; leaflets, pamphlets, books and training materials.

WALES COUNCIL FOR VOLUNTARY ACTION

Address Llys Ifor, Crescent Road, Caerphilly, Mid Glamorgan CF8 1XL
Tel Caerphilly 869 224

Organisation Formerly the Council of Social Service for Wales, an independent national organisation established to promote, support and facilitate voluntary action and community development in Wales. The Council provides through the work of its staff and committees a service of advice and consultancy to all voluntary organisations which seek assistance; an intelligence service by monitoring developments in the voluntary sector in Wales and throughout the UK, government policies and current trends in society; an educational programme through the provision of a range of educational events from conferences to workshops; a representational role by responding to government consultations, taking the initiative to bring into the forum of public debate issues of importance for the development of voluntary action in Wales; a particular support system for voluntary sponsors of MSC schemes; and assists in the development of new projects which will link voluntary, statutory and commercial resources towards work creation and new forms of community benefit. Acts as an agency for support of other important voluntary innovations or services such as Opportunities for Volunteering.

Advice The information service directly responds to enquiries from institutions on voluntary organisations in Wales.

Publications *Network Wales* monthly newsletter; *County Directories of Voluntary Organisations*; *A Short Guide to Voluntary Work Opportunities in Wales* information sheet; Annual Report; booklets; guides; reports.

SECTION VI

PRACTICAL INFORMATION

PRACTICAL INFORMATION

Preparation Thorough preparation is vital for the success of any project; in addition to obtaining information and any studies that volunteers may carry out for themselves, the agency should offer an orientation course providing a greater understanding of the service conditions and the social, economic and political situation in the country of destination, and, depending on the assignment, further training. This may not take place entirely before the volunteer leaves for the project, and ideally it should continue throughout the period of service; to receive up-to-date information volunteers are recommended to write to those already on the project, which will have the added benefit of establishing a personal contact for arrival. If the volunteer has been accepted by an overseas organisation unable to provide an orientation course in the UK, a number of agencies and other organisations arrange specialist residential briefing courses for those about to go overseas:

ACTION HEALTH 2000 35 Bird Farm Road, Fulbourn, Cambridge CB1 5DP Tel Cambridge 880194
An international voluntary health association working for better health care in the Third World by creating greater awareness of the issues involved and giving practical support to appropriate health programmes. Organise a weekend orientation course for health personnel and development workers planning to work in the Third World, covering health and development, country briefings, personal health care and survival, travel, insurance, fundraising and communication skills. Opportunity to meet and talk with those who have worked in the Third World.

THE CENTRE FOR INTERNATIONAL BRIEFING The Castle, Farnham, Surrey GU9 0AG Tel Farnham 721194
A non-profit educational organisation providing 4-day residential briefing courses for those, including volunteers, who have been appointed to work in the developing countries of Africa, Latin America and the Caribbean, Asia and the Pacific, and the Middle East. The courses provide an understanding of the working environment and cover the culture, values and attitudes, history, the political, social and economic structure, current affairs, future trends and living conditions of the destination country.
Also arrange courses on Britain for those from overseas who have recently arrived to take up residence, especially on professional development assignments.

TEAR FUND Administrator Overseas Personnel, 100 Church Road, Teddington, Middlesex TW11 8QE Tel 01-977 9144
Organise orientation courses for Christian volunteers who have been accepted to serve overseas. The courses last for 2 weeks, and are usually held in April, September and December. All Nations College and Worldwide Evangelisation Crusade lecturers, ex-volunteers and videos are used to brief participants on development, economic situations, inter-personal and spiritual matters, and health care.

VOLUNTEER MISSIONARY MOVEMENT Shenley Lane, London Colney, Hertfordshire AL2 1AR Tel Bowmansgreen 24853
An ecumenical movement within the Catholic Church which recruits, prepares and sends Christian volunteers with a skill or profession to work as lay missionaries in projects linked with local churches. Organise and run a 5-

week residential preparation course to help those who are going overseas to reflect upon and examine their motivation and to provide them with relevant up-to-date information. The course covers all aspects of life and work overseas and participants learn about the people with whom they will be working and the countries and projects in which they will work. Underlying the course is the missionary element, with special emphasis placed on prayer, spiritual formation and guidance; returned volunteers share their experiences.

Training Adapting existing skills and learning new ones may be essential for the work the volunteers are going to do; the agency will probably explain in detail how the volunteers' skills will be utilised. If volunteers are to communicate effectively with local people they should be able to speak the language, and basic language instruction before departure and conversation classes on arrival are practical methods of surmounting communication obstacles; many agencies arrange language instruction or will advise on suitable classes elsewhere.

The *Resource Directory* is an excellent source of information for those with or needing specialist skills. It is divided into eight sections, each containing details of related training courses, agencies and publications: development; relief/disaster/refugees; health; water/sanitation; agriculture; technology; logistics; and recruitment/orientation. Published by World Vision of Europe, 146 Queen Victoria Street, London EC4 4BX.

Development in the Rural Space is a booklet containing details of the principal UK development courses on agriculture, education, health/nutrition/population, planning/management/administration and technology. Published by the British Council, 10 Spring Gardens, London SW1A 1BH.

ApT DESIGN AND DEVELOPMENT 28-30 Northwick Park, Blockley, Moreton-in-Marsh, Gloucestershire GL56 9RF
A charity providing technical assistance to small-scale workshops in developing countries, offering potential volunteers the benefit of experience overseas including the reduction of reliance on sophisticated machines in favour of improvisation and ingenuity, enabling the volunteer to teach people to make their own workshop equipment. They train people in metalworking techniques and in the construction of ApT-developed equipment; projects to date have been in Bangladesh, Botswana, Chile, India, Iran, Kenya, Malawi, Sri Lanka, Venezuela and Zimbabwe.

Understanding development
There is a certain amount of controversy about the extent to which the industrialised nations are responsible for the underdevelopment of the Third World and about what steps should be taken to effect a change in the relationship. The prospective volunteer can find out more about these issues and the situation in the developing countries from the following organisations.
Note that none recruits volunteers, but all produce a range of useful literature.

AMNESTY INTERNATIONAL BRITISH SECTION 5 Roberts Place, off Bowling Green Lane, London EC1 OEJ Tel 01-251 8371
A voluntarily financed worldwide human rights movement which is independent of any government, political faction, ideology, economic interest or religious creed. It works for the release of prisoners of conscience provided they have never used or advocated violence, advocates fair and early trials for all political prisoners, and opposes the death penalty and torture or other cruel, inhuman or degrading treatment of all prisoners without reservation. Annual *Amnesty International*

Report details its work and main concerns in more than 120 countries and has a factual country-by-country account of human rights abuses; *Country Reports*; *Theme Reports*.

APPROPRIATE HEALTH RESOURCES AND TECHNOLOGIES ACTION GROUP 85 Marylebone High Street, London W1M 3DE Tel 01-486 4175

A charity which aims to promote primary health care in developing countries and to encourage the development of appropriate health technologies offering alternatives to high cost medical practice. Library and resource centre available to health workers going to work in developing countries; contains a wide range of relevant books, journals, documents, information packs and regularly updated bibliographies and training information. *Publications List* includes newsletters, resource lists, briefing packs and directories covering primary health care.

CATHOLIC FUND FOR OVERSEAS DEVELOPMENT 2 Garden Close, Stockwell Road, London SW9 9TY Tel 01-733 7900

The official Catholic Church agency for overseas development aiming to increase awareness of poverty and injustice in the world and the structures which cause them. Supports over 400 projects in community development, vocational training, preventive health care, food production, water development and non-formal education in some 70 Third World countries. *Resources Catalogue* lists general books and materials, simulation games, country profiles, and campaign, theology, social teaching and liturgical material.

CENTRE FOR WORLD DEVELOPMENT EDUCATION 128 Buckingham Palace Road, London SW1W 9SH Tel 01-730 8332

An independent agency whose main aim is to promote education in Britain about world development issues and Britain's interdependence with the Third World; funded partly by the Overseas Development Administration. Annual *Catalogue* includes a wide range of handbooks, guides, booklets, information sheets and other materials on world development and interdependence; employment, technology, industry and energy; EC and the Third World; aid, disasters and refugees; immigrants and migration; population and education; and health, food and agriculture.

CHRISTIAN AID PO Box 1, London SW9 8BH Tel 01-733 5500

The overseas aid division of the British Council of Churches, helping those victimised by poverty and the abuse of power to change their circumstances and prospects. It uses its resources for projects which contribute to the well-being and self-reliance of people, and assists in building up the life of the churches overseas so that they may more effectively serve their communities. *Publications & Visual Aids Catalogue* includes background resources, material on exiles and migrants, worship and study, simulation games and activities, and other sources of materials and advice.

COUNCIL FOR EDUCATION IN WORLD CITIZENSHIP 19/21 Tudor Street, London EC4Y 0DJ Tel 01-353 3353

A non-political and non-sectarian organisation promoting through the education system such studies and teachings as may best contribute to mutual understanding, peace and cooperation, and goodwill between all peoples. Regular *Broadsheets* provide authoritative and up-to-date background information on countries and issues in the news; *World Studies Resource Guide* lists over 100 organisations in the fields of international affairs, world poverty, race relations, volunteering, politics, schools and the community; resource guides, books/booklets and fact sheets.

EARTHSCAN 3 Endsleigh Street, London WC1H 0DD Tel 01-388 9541

An international institute providing a news and information service on environment and development issues, aimed mainly at the media, non-governmental organisations and government and development agencies. *Catalogue* lists paperbacks on the misuse of natural resources and Third World development, and technical reports on Third World energy technologies. Areas covered include natural disasters, wildlife/conservation, forests, deserts/agriculture, climate, architecture/planning, water and energy.

INTERMEDIATE TECHNOLOGY DEVELOPMENT GROUP Myson House, Railway Terrace, Rugby CV21 3HT Tel Rugby 60631

Dedicated to increasing the income-generating capabilities of poor people in rural areas of the developing world by providing information, advice and assistance on the choice of appropriate technologies which make the best use of readily available local skills and resources, and minimises the demands on scarce and imported resources. Publications include titles on policy and economics; agriculture and fish culture; building and construction; cooperatives; education; energy sources; gardening and nutrition; health; industry and business; roads and transport; water supply and sanitation; source books; and occasional papers.

MINORITY RIGHTS GROUP 29 Craven Street, London WC2N 5NT Tel 01-930 6659

An international human rights organisation investigating a whole range of minority and majority situations in the world arising from discrimination and prejudice. Works through the UN and other international bodies to increase awareness of human rights issues, and fosters international understanding of the factors which create prejudiced treatment and group tensions, helping to promote the growth of a world conscience regarding human rights. Has 69 *Reports* on the problems of a wide range of oppressed groups in Africa, the Americas, Asia, Southern Oceans, Middle East and Europe.

NATIONAL ASSOCIATION OF DEVELOPMENT EDUCATION CENTRES 128 Buckingham Palace Road, London SW1W 9SH Tel 01-730 0972

Assists and advises organisations engaged in setting up/running development education centres, and provides a channel to communicate information and views to government bodies concerned with development, non-governmental organisations and the general public. Produce regularly up-dated lists of development education centres and a monthly newsletter providing prospective volunteers with a forum for discussion and a source of background information on the developing countries.

THIRD WORLD FIRST 232 Cowley Road, Oxford OX4 1UH Tel Oxford 245678

A national movement in colleges and universities, explaining and campaigning against the causes of poverty, hunger and exploitation in the Third World, and supporting the growing efforts of the poor as they organise together to determine their own development. *Publications List* covers books and fact sheets on world development issues including health, women, aid, disarmament, racism and environment.

THIRD WORLD PUBLICATIONS 151 Stratford Road, Birmingham B11 1RD Tel 021-773 6572

A non-profit workers' cooperative providing a wide range of books and pamphlets from and about the Third World. Areas covered include Africa, the Americas, Middle East, Asia, Third World life, women, and black and Arabic literature.

UK COMMITTEE FOR UNICEF
55 Lincoln's Inn Fields, London WC2A 3NB Tel 01-405 5592
UNICEF is an integral but semi-autonomous part of the UN, addressing the problems of children in the developing world, serving 117 countries and working in social services, nutrition, emergency relief and rehabilitation, water/sanitation, primary health care and formal/non-formal education. *The State of the World's Children* reports on the progress of strategies for child survival, and the simple and low-cost methods that could bring about a dramatic improvement in the well-being of the world's children. Produces books, information packs and study materials.

WAR ON WANT Three Castles House, 1 London Bridge Street, London SE1 9UT Tel 01-403 2266
International aid agency actively campaigning against injustice and oppression in developing countries and for increasing awareness in the UK of the causes of world poverty. Funds long-term and emergency relief in famine areas torn by military struggle, where little international aid is sent.
Publications List covers titles concerned with health, child care, women, famine, developmental issues, politics, exploitation and oppression.

WORLD DEVELOPMENT MOVEMENT Bedford Chambers, Covent Garden, London WC2E 8HA Tel 01-836 3672
Campaigns for changes in Britain's policies that affect poor countries, and for reforms in world trade, finance and agriculture to resolve the underlying causes of poverty, famine and disease. *Publications List* covers aid, food, EC and the Third World, North-South issues, energy, medicines and tobacco, and disarmament and development.

Passports It is essential to check that your passport is valid at least for the time you intend to stay overseas and, as your circumstances and intentions may change, it is wise to allow an extra 6 months. Immigration and other government officials usually turn to a new page when stamping passports, so check that there are enough clear pages for visas and stamps; the British Passport Office issues a 94 page passport which is useful for those travelling through several countries. Another point to remember is that entry stamps for Israel, Cuba, South Africa and Taiwan may make it impossible to enter some other countries; authorities in these countries usually agree not to stamp your passport if asked, but check before departure in case the situation has changed. Always apply well in advance for a passport, especially prior to the holiday season; a standard UK passport costs £15 (£22.50 if particulars of family are included), the larger size costs £30. Both are valid for 10 years and are obtainable from the following regional offices:

Passport Office, Clive House, 70-78 Petty France, London SW1H 9HD
Tel 01-213 3344/3434/6161/7272

Passport Office, 5th Floor, India Buildings, Water Street, Liverpool L2 0QZ Tel 051-237 3010

Passport Office, Olympia House, Upper Dock Street, Newport, Gwent NPT 1XA Tel Newport 56292

Passport Office, 55 Westfield Road, Peterborough, Cambridgeshire PE3 6TG Tel Peterborough 895555

Passport Office, 1st Floor, Empire House, 131 West Nile Street, Glasgow G1 2RY Tel 041-332 0271

Passport Office, Hampton House, 47-53 High Street, Belfast BT1 2QS Tel 0232-232371

Essential information for holders of UK passports who intend to travel overseas is a booklet containing notes on illness or injury while abroad, insurance, vaccinations, NHS medical cards, consular assistance overseas, British Customs and other useful advice; available free from all Passport Offices and post offices.

Visas An increasing number of countries require visas; the recruiting agency should inform you on entry and exit visa procedures, but volunteers are strongly advised to check for themselves whether they need a visa, that they have obtained the correct one and that it is valid for the length of time they expect to be in the country. As the visa application process can be a lengthy one, allow plenty of time; visa application details are available from the consular section of the appropriate embassy, and current information on worldwide visa regulations can be found in the quarterly *ABC Guide to International Travel* published by ABC Travel Guides, World Timetable Centre, Church Street, Dunstable, Bedfordshire LU5 4HB.

Medical requirements It is wise to have medical and dental check-ups well before departure; treatment may be expensive and difficult to obtain in the country of destination. British Embassies and Consulates can provide a list of local English-speaking doctors which can be helpful if you do need treatment. A letter from your doctor can prevent trouble with the authorities if, for health reasons, you have to carry prescribed drugs; to ensure that you will be able to find a particular medicine when overseas find out its generic name, as brand names for drugs vary from country to country. If you wear spectacles take a spare pair and make a note of the prescription in case you lose or break them; contact lenses can prove to be painful and hard to keep clean in dusty regions, in which case you may consider changing to spectacles.

Immunisation Immunisation should be started well in advance as some courses necessitate an interval between the first and second inoculation, or between one immunisation and another; with vaccination against yellow fever, for example, there must be an interval of at least 21 days before any other vaccination with a live virus, such as polio. As immunity may not develop for several days, validity may not be immediate; immigration officials will not accept a yellow fever immunisation certificate until 10 days after the vaccination. In addition, should you suffer after-effects, it would be wise to recover before leaving, rather than suffer during the journey and the first crucial days on the project. Although yellow fever and cholera immunisations may be mandatory for particular countries, some recommended immunisations may be even more important for the protection of your health than the mandatory ones. These are likely to be typhoid, tetanus, particularly important in the tropics, polio, hepatitis, which many agencies insist their volunteers are immunised against, rabies, for those at special risk such as vets and zoologists, and malaria, for which prophylactic pills are necessary. Some vaccinations are free under the National Health Service, but for others there may be a charge and doctors can charge for signing or filling in a vaccination certificate. Preventive measures to be taken against these diseases are modified frequently, particularly in the case of malaria, and your local doctor may not have all the current information; for up to date advice consult:

Birmingham Unit for Communicable Disease and Tropical Medicine, East Birmingham Hospital, Bordesley Green East, Birmingham B9 5ST Tel 021-772 4311

The Communicable Diseases (Scotland) Unit, Ruchill Hospital, Bilsland Drive, Glasgow G20 9NB Tel 041-946 7120

The Liverpool School of Tropical Medicine, Pembroke Place, Liverpool L3 5QA Tel 051-708 9393

The London School of Hygiene and Tropical Medicine, Keppel Street, London WC1E 7HD Tel 01-636 8636

Public Health Laboratory Service, Communicable Disease Surveillance Centre, 61 Colindale Avenue, London NW9 5EQ Tel 01-200 6868

The Department of Health and Social Security publishes a leaflet *SA35, Protect Your Health Abroad* which contains vital information for people travelling overseas, especially to hotter climates. It details compulsory and recommended vaccinations and what else can be done to protect your health overseas, and gives information on yellow fever, cholera, infectious hepatitis, typhoid, tetanus, polio, malaria and rabies, precautions to be taken against contracting these diseases, a list of countries where they can be contracted, and action to take in an emergency.
There is advice on types of food and on water supplies which may be a source of infection; a list of yellow fever vaccination centres in the UK is also given. Available free from the Department of Health and Social Security, International Relations Division, Alexander Fleming House, Elephant and Castle, London SE1 6BY Tel 01-407 5522 ext 6749.

The following centres can provide vaccination at short notice, but charge for the service:

British Airways Immunisation Centre, 75 Regent Street, London W1 Tel 01-439 9584

British Airways Medical Centre, Terminal 3, Heathrow Airport Tel 01-759 5511 ext 2301

PPP Medical Centre, 99 New Cavendish Street, London W1 Tel 01-637 8941

Thomas Cook, 45 Berkeley Street, London W1 Tel 01-499 4000

Useful guides to health care overseas include:

The Tropical Traveller by John Hatt, published by Pan Books, Cavaye Place, London SW10 9PG.

The Traveller's Health Book by Dr Anthony Turner, published by Roger Lascelles, 44 York Road, Brentford, Middlesex.

A Health Handbook for the Tropics by Dr Gervase Hamilton, written for volunteers and available from Voluntary Service Overseas, 9 Belgrave Square, London SW1X 8PW.

Medical treatment You are only covered by the NHS while in the UK, and will usually have to pay the full costs of treatment abroad. However, there are health care arrangements with all the European Community (EC) countries (Belgium, Denmark, France, Federal Republic of Germany, Greece, Ireland, Italy, Luxembourg, Netherlands, Portugal and Spain) and in addition there are reciprocal health care arrangements with Austria, Bulgaria, the Channel Islands, Czechoslovakia, German Democratic Republic, Finland, Gibraltar, Hong Kong, Hungary, Iceland, Isle of Man, Malta, New Zealand, Norway, Poland, Portugal, Romania, Sweden, USSR, Yugoslavia and British Dependent Territories of Anguilla, British Virgin Islands, Falkland Islands, Montserrat, St Helena and Turks and Caicos Islands. Leaflet *SA30, Medical Costs Abroad*, available from local offices of the Department of Health and Social Security (DHSS), details the procedures necessary to qualify for free or reduced cost medical treatment in the EC and these countries. It includes details of what treatment is free or at reduced cost, circumstances in which you should retain your NHS medical card, and those where no official documents other than a passport are usually needed. Private medical insurance is recommended to cover the cost of repatriation and additional medical expenses not covered under the arrangements.

If you are about to undertake a period of voluntary service in either an EC country or one of the countries with which there is a reciprocal health care arrangement, you should write to the DHSS, Overseas Branch, Newcastle upon Tyne NE98 1YX, giving your full name and UK address, overseas address, if known, national insurance or pension number, your proposed date of departure and the name and address of the employer.

It has not proved possible to make arrangements for UK passport holders to receive free or reduced cost medical treatment in any other countries than those mentioned above, so it is strongly advised that volunteers going to those countries take out adequate private medical insurance.

If you are coming to the UK for a period of voluntary service you should contact the relevant government department in your country for details of any reciprocal health arrangements.

Insurance It is in your own interests to have adequate insurance, not only for medical treatment, but also life and personal accident cover and to cover cash and possessions. Many volunteer agencies provide some insurance but this is often solely against third party risks and accidents, and in this case you would need to supplement the provision. Existing insurance policies may already cover the insured at home and overseas, but may need extending to cover the nature of the situations volunteers will find themselves in. It is common to include cover in the policy for ambulance transport, and in certain circumstance repatriation, including medical attention on the journey and the conveyance of a relative or friend. Cover for personal effects should include baggage in transit and at destination, and expensive individual items, for example, like photographic equipment. Volunteers should carefully check the limit for the total package as well as for each claim, that the policy does cover them for the type of work they will be doing, and whether there is a representative of the insurance company in the destination country to whom claims can be made.

Whatever the insurance cover purchased, the policy should be thoroughly examined, its limits and exclusion clauses established, and a copy taken with you. If a claim on the policy arises, the insurance company should be informed with the fullest details, without delay, and where a crime is involved the local police need also to be notified.

It can prove difficult to arrange insurance cover for extended overseas periods;.policies can be bought from insurance companies, insurance brokers or travel agents, and Lloyd's Advisory Department, London House, 6 London Street, London EC3R 7AV Tel 01-623 7100 can recommend a broker, advise on insurance claims and provide general information.

National Insurance The regulations covering National Insurance contributions and social security are complex and become more complicated for those paying contributions while overseas. Your entitlement to sickness, invalidity and uneployment benefit, maternity allowance, and state pension is governed by your National Insurance record, but this does not affect entitlement to other social security benefits such as supplementary benefit. Those agencies which are members of the British Volunteer Programme pay

National Insurance contributions automatically for their volunteers, but whichever organisation you are working with it is essential to clarify the position regarding National Insurance contributions well in advance of taking up a volunteer post; neglecting to make proper arrangements may well prejudice any future claims for benefits.

If you are going to one of the EC countries, leaflet *SA29, Your Social Security and Pension Rights in the European Community* available from the Department of Health and Social Security Overseas Branch *see below*, gives details of National Insurance contributions, plus the social security rights available to UK nationals and how and where to claim them.

If you are going outside the EC, there are separate leaflets detailing social security procedures in countries where the UK has a reciprocal arrangement: Australia, Austria, Bermuda, Canada, Cyprus, Finland, Isle of Man, Israel, Jamaica, Jersey and Guernsey, Malta, Mauritius, New Zealand, Norway, Switzerland, Turkey, USA (agreement affects British retirement pensioners only) and Yugoslavia. For other countries, leaflet *NI38, Social Security Abroad* applies. For further information write to DHSS Overseas Branch, Newcastle upon Tyne, NE98 1YX.

Regulations are to be introduced by the British Government to comply with the EC Council recommendation on social security for volunteer development workers which was adopted in June 1985. The result will be a modification of existing National Insurance contribution regulations, ensuring that all volunteer development workers going overseas will be entitled to the full range of benefits on their return, whether or not they receive more than the lower earnings limit from their organisation. For precise information on these changes contact DHSS, 151 Great Titchfield

Street, London W1P 8AD
Tel 01-636 1696 ext 50.

If you live outside the UK you should contact the relevant government department in your country for advice.

Social security and volunteering in the UK If you are unemployed and intend to volunteer in the UK you should consult DHSS leaflet *NI240, Voluntary Work and Social Security Benefits*. You can only undertake voluntary work within your usual main occupation *and* continue to claim benefit if the work is for a charity, local authority or health authority.
Normally, to qualify as available for work, you must be available to attend for interview or take up a job at 24 hours notice, and residential work will affect your availability; in any case, you must obtain permission to volunteer from your local DHSS office.
Volunteers on unemployment benefit may earn up to £2 per day without losing benefit, excluding Sundays when there is no earnings limit; those on supplementary benefit may earn up to £4 per week without losing benefit. These figures exclude certain allowable expenses.

Travel One travel agency which complements the theme of this book, as its profits are paid into a trust fund for the assignment of aid to projects in the poorest areas of the Third World, is North-South Travel Ltd, Room 1A, 6 Brondesbury Road, London NW6 6AS Tel 01-624 4416. It arranges competitively priced, reliably planned flights to most parts of the world, and in addition to providing travel information regarding countries in which volunteers are working, holds meetings for volunteers and produces reports containing news and comments sent in by volunteers from areas in which they are engaged.

Practical tips can be gleaned from *The Tropical Traveller* by John Hatt

published by Pan Books Ltd, Cavaye Place, London SW10 9PG.

ABC Guide to International Travel published by ABC Travel Guides, World Timetable Centre, Church Street, Dunstable, Bedfordshire LU5 4HB will provide you with detailed travel information and regulations.

The Traveller's Handbook published by Futura Publications in association with WEXAS International, 45 Brompton Road, London SW3, is an indispensable guide to trouble-free travel.

Always double check your travel details such as flight number, time of departure and Customs regulations; it is very easy to forget small but important things, for example airport and departure taxes may be payable in a particular currency, so ascertain whether the taxes are included in the ticket price and, if not, in what currency they are payable.

Emergencies It is worth checking before you leave what support, if any, your organisation can give you in times of emergency or trouble. The consular offices at British Embassies in overseas capitals and at Consulates in some provincial cities can offer help; you should look up the address, telephone and telex number of the one you will be nearest to in the *Diplomatic Service List*, which should be in your local library. If the consul's urgent help is needed it is usually better to telephone or telegraph your message rather than send a letter; the telegraphic address of all British Embassies is *Prodrome* and of all British Consulates, *Britain*, followed in each case by the name of the town. Consuls will advise or help in cases of serious difficulty or distress; they cannot give advice on, or pay for, legal proceedings but will do what they can to help in such cases. As a last resort they can arrange for a direct return to the UK by the cheapest possible passage, providing you agree to have your passport withdrawn and give written confirmation that you will pay for the travel expenses involved on return. If a passport is lost or stolen while abroad, the local police should be notified immediately; if necessary the nearest British Embassy or Consulate will issue a substitute.

Before you go overseas, make sure that you have the following information which you should keep separate from your other belongings: passport number, date and place of issue; air/rail/boat ticket numbers, dates and places of issue; insurance details and 24 hour emergency number; local agency representative details; Embassy or Consulate information; serial numbers of travellers cheques; any medical prescriptions.

Returning A few months before the end of the assignment volunteers should begin to prepare themselves for the return home; the agency should be ready to help and advise on re-establishment, and the volunteer should request information while still overseas if they have not received any advice. Many volunteers find the culture shock of returning home equal to that of going; those who come back not expecting to meet practical problems concerning health, housing, employment and state benefits can find themselves under great stress.

As indicated in the entries, most agencies arrange debriefing; in some cases this can be perfunctory, but agencies who are genuinely concerned with their overseas development workers will give them the opportunity to engage in constructive evaluation of the project. This is really the first part of utilising the experiences gained overseas effectively; by pointing out successful methods, drawing attention to failures and describing the conditions, the volunteers' reports and comments may be able to aid the agency in its work in the future.

If it is offered, volunteers should take up the opportunity to participate in briefing courses for prospective volunteers, providing an alternative reference point to judge things by and an excellent opportunity to apply what has been learnt abroad to life and work in the home country. There are many organisations working towards educating people about development and changing the way the industrialised nations behave in their relations with the Third World, which volunteers can join; see the Understanding Development section. Further help and advice on reorientation and continuing commitment can be obtained from the following organisations:

RETURNED VOLUNTEER ACTION 1 Amwell Street, London EC1R 1UL Tel 01-278 0804
An organisation of, and for, returned volunteers, those interested or active in development work, and others who have worked overseas. It believes that a period of voluntary service overseas fails to achieve its full value unless it becomes part of an educative process for the volunteer, and most of its work involves face-to-face contact between more recently returned volunteers and those who have been back for up to 2 years. Its main aims are to press for improvements in the volunteer programme and help returned volunteers evaluate their overseas experience, using the understanding which that experience has given them in development education, community action and other fields in the UK.

Organises Questioning Development days for prospective volunteers, where they can talk to returned volunteers in informal discussion sessions. Practical advice and support is provided in reorientation weekends; other conferences on development education themes are held from time to time, and returned volunteers are helped in their search for work in the UK with the Jobsheet which is in the members' quarterly magazine *Comeback*. Members participate in local activities wherever they can and in many areas have themselves taken initiatives in starting development-oriented activities.

In the area of volunteer policy work, RVA participates in the British Volunteer Programme council and maintains close contact with the BVP agencies. A link is provided with volunteers in Europe and further afield through Ex-Volunteers International, which holds conferences exchanging ideas on new directions and development education. In addition to its Volunteer Policy, Development Education and Women's Groups, it actively supports small development projects overseas through a Development Fund. **BVP**

Publishes a range of titles including *Working Overseas* advisory pack containing information on the sending agencies and general advice for the prospective overseas worker/volunteer; *Questioning Development*; *Handbook for Development Workers Overseas*; *Thinking About Volunteering*; *EVI Charter*; *Poverty and Power*.

COMHLAMH 4/5 Eustace Street, Dublin 2 Tel Dublin 716795
The Returned Development Workers' Association of Ireland aims to maintain friendship and partnership with the peoples of the developing countries; to contribute to a greater awareness on the part of the Irish people of the problems of developing countries and of solutions required; to assist returning development workers with their readjustment to life in Ireland and in obtaining or resuming employment; and to assist them to contribute effectively from their experience to social and community development in Ireland. Its activities are carried out through

local branches and groups that focus on distinct development issues. The Services' Group in particular helps returned development workers by providing them with reorientation weekends, communications skills courses, practical guidance concerning jobs, retraining and social welfare benefits and information about possibilities for development work in Ireland.
Publishes *Comhlamh News* quarterly magazine.

AVEC 155a Kings Road, Chelsea, London SW3 5TX Tel 01-352 2033
A service agency for church and community work which organises residential courses, sponsored by the Methodist Church Overseas Division, for missionaries returning to work in the UK and Ireland. Open to ordained and lay people of all denominations, the courses provide opportunities to reflect on what has been learnt from missionary experience and to draw out the practical and theological implications for the work to be taken up in the UK and for the sponsoring missionary organisation.

Publications Throughout this guide details have been given of where further information can be found; the following publications provide additional information on voluntary service:

Guide to Voluntary Work Opportunities compiled by Carolyn Oldfield and Louise Bulman; lists national and local agencies offering part-time, short and long-term volunteer opportunities in the UK. Areas of work include: archaeology, children and young people, Christian communities, community action, conservation and environment, counselling, elderly, handicapped, homeless, mental health, rights, workcamps. Published by the National Youth Bureau, 17-23 Albion Street, Leicester LE1 6GD.

The International Directory of Voluntary Work edited by David

Woodworth, is a guide to 400 agencies and sources of information on short to long-term voluntary work in the UK and worldwide. Published by Vacation Work, 9 Park End Street, Oxford OX1 1HJ.

Invest Yourself is an annual catalogue of volunteer opportunities with 190 non-governmental organisations in North America and worldwide, including articles on the volunteer experience. Published by the Commission on Voluntary Service and Action, PO Box 117, New York, NY 10009, USA.

Volunteer! by Marjorie Adoff Cohen. A guide to voluntary service containing details of 175 voluntary service organisations with opportunities mainly in the USA and on international workcamps. Published jointly by the Council on International Educational Exchange and the Commission on Voluntary Service and Action. Available from Intercultural Press, PO Box 768, Yarmouth, Maine 04096, United States of America.

Volunteering in Literacy Work lists volunteer opportunities in the struggle to eliminate illiteracy. Areas of work include initial literacy teaching, post-literacy programmes to help maintain newly learnt skills, preparation of literacy materials, and fundraising for literacy campaigns. Published in cooperation with the UNESCO Literacy, Adult Education and Rural Development Division by the Coordinating Committee for International Voluntary Service, 1 rue Miollis, 75015 Paris, France.

Volunteering Opportunities in Scotland lists volunteer opportunities in conservation, workcamps, community projects, playschemes and hospitals, useful advice on setting up a community project, a listing of volunteer bureaux in Scotland and useful publications. Published by the Scottish Community Education Council, Atholl House, 2 Canning Street, Edinburgh EH3 8EG.

Resource Directory is an excellent source of information on areas related to relief and development work in developing countries, containing details of British and international agencies, related training courses and publications. Published by World Vision of Europe, 146 Queen Victoria Street, London EC4 4BX.

SECTION VII

INDEXES

COUNTRIES INDEX

ORGANISATIONS INDEX

PROJECTS INDEX

VOLUNTEER WORK REPORT FORM

Up to date reports of volunteering opportunities enable us to improve the accuracy and standard of the information in this guide. It would be appreciated if, after a period of voluntary service, volunteers could complete and return this report form form to the Information Department, Central Bureau for Educational Visits and Exchanges, Seymour Mews House, Seymour Mews, London W1H 9PE. **All reports will be treated in strict confidence.**

Name and address of organisation concerned

Location of project/work

Type of work undertaken

Qualifications/skills necessary

Length of service

What was the length of time between application and departure?

What was the selection procedure?

What orientation was provided?

Was the orientation a satisfactory briefing?

Were you given any training to help adapt your skills to the post?

Was travel and insurance provided?

If you had to make any financial contribution, was help given with finding sponsorship?

Did you find that personnel at headquarters were genuinely concerned with your welfare?

Did they respond quickly to your reports and requests?

How did the aims of the agency match up to their actions in the field?

What preparations had been made for you before you arrived?

What type of board and accommodation was provided?

How adequately were you occupied during the assignment?

What was the relationship between your organisation and local people?

Do you think that volunteers are really needed in the project?

What help/advice was given to you on return?

Would you recommend this volunteer opportunity?

Any other comments

Signed   **Date**

Name

Age

Home address